Communication

Authenticity

Respect

Enjoyment

Communication

Authenticity

Respect

Enjoyment

PEOPLE PEOPLE

PEOPLE PEOPLE

WHO they are.

WHY they win.

HOW to be one.

Scott Christopher

GIBBS SMITH

TO ENRICH AND INSPIRE HUMANKIND

*Dedicated to my little group of extraordinary People People: Liz, Christian,
Joshua, Matthew, Scott and John, without whom I probably wouldn't
bother leaving the house every day, much less writing another book.*

First Edition
17 16 15 14 13   5 4 3 2 1

Text © 2013 Scott Christopher

Published by
Gibbs Smith
P.O. Box 667
Layton, Utah 84041

1.800.835.4993 orders
www.gibbs-smith.com

Designed by Kurt Wahlner

Gibbs Smith books are printed on paper produced from sustainable PEFC-
certified forest/controlled wood source. Learn more at www.pefc.org.
Printed and bound in Hong Kong

Library of Congress Cataloging-in-Publication Data

Christopher, Scott, 1967–
  People people / Scott Christopher. — First edition.
     pages cm
  Includes bibliographical references.
  ISBN 978-1-4236-3303-7
1. Success. 2. Success in business. 3. Interpersonal relations. 4.
Caring. I. Title.
  BF637.S8C475 2013
  650.1—dc23
                    2012044609

Contents

Acknowledgments

This work would not have been possible without the support, ideas and contributions of James Claflin and Elizabeth Claflin. Adrian Gostick, Chester Elton, Steve Gibbons and the many talented minds at The Culture Works have long been an inspiration in my creative processes. Thanks are also due to the good people at Ultimate Software, Marriott International, Camden Property Trust, New Belgium Brewing, ESL Federal Credit Union, Glassdoor and Scottrade. Special thanks to Bob Cooper and the entire Gibbs Smith team. A very personal thanks to Lillian Tyler for her absolute lifelong embodiment of a true T3 People Person.

CHAPTER ONE
An Introduction to People People

Leonardo da Vinci once said, "Simplicity is the ultimate sophistication." Albert Einstein said that if you can't explain something to a six-year-old, then you don't understand it yourself. Occam's razor states that the simplest answer is usually the right one. Still, a simpleton like me worries that it's oversimplifying to say, and it pains me to write this, that this book is about *being nice*.

You may have just cringed a little. I know I did.

Other very successful authors and researchers have published seminal works on "nice," and it is not my intention either to add to or subtract (but definitely steal) from the body of work they've contributed to the topic. For one thing, I am neither a *successful* author nor a very good researcher.

I wanted to write a true self-help book—one that would help *me*. Because something you must understand first and foremost is that I am *not* a People Person. Sure, I possess certain characteristics that are traditional to People People like affability and a firm handshake, and I'm a bit fun loving (as evidenced by the cover photo), but as you'll discover in the following pages, there's a lot more to it than just being a bit extroverted.

I've approached this topic from a more personal perspective than other books I've written, sharing truths that I've discovered in my various career iterations. Or maybe they're not altogether "truths." Perhaps they're just my opinions and what I personally consider to be truths. Either way, you're stuck with the book now, so you may as well accept them as truths. (Trust me, it'll make the reading seem less tedious.) Rest assured, this is not entirely an autobiographical, whimsical collection of anecdotes and experience. I have mingled some data and relevant business examples into the argument as well.

People People are nice people, truly nice people. Not temporary, "how will it benefit me to be nice?" people. But people who *care* . . . about business—sure; about pleasing clients—absolutely; about doing excellent work—of course. But more to the point: people who *genuinely care* about other people.

I hope you'll indulge me the following reminiscences here; my intent is to provide some context, frame the argument, set the stage, lay the table and fill the tub.

Watching Scotty Grow

I was born in Michigan and my parents divorced when I was still a baby. Without a father in the home, life was difficult for the four of us kids (two boys, two girls) and our mother, Lillian. She was committed to being an at-home, traditional mother to the greatest possible extent, often sacrificing well-paying work so she could be there for us in the mornings and after school. She chose to forgo the luxuries that pursuing a full-time career might provide, rather than raise us in absentia, even if that sometimes meant living in government housing projects, small apartments or other humble quarters. But we were happy enough, and I have fond memories of those simple, hand-to-mouth days. I had some interesting friends growing up, to say the least, and the neighborhood games and goofing off lasted late into the night.

But as with all kids, especially boys it seems, I needed the role model, love, security and balance that a father in the home can provide. Many good men from our neighborhood and church would invite me to join them and their kids on campouts and fishing and hunting outings. Usually two men from the church would visit our home at least monthly to assess how we were doing and provide material help when times were tight, which wasn't infrequently. Christmases were always highlighted by sweet acts of service and charity, as caring people would often anonymously leave foods, treats or gifts at our doorstep. They would help get me involved in Boy Scouts and other youth activities to provide discipline, direction and preparation for adult life.

As Mom tried to find a suitable man for both her and us, the occasional nutjob would surface. One such was a college professor that rubbed all four of us kids the wrong way. He was a bit stern, quite creepy, a neat freak and stereotypically nerdy. Though we didn't really mind that *some* guy would take our dad's place at home, we certainly didn't want it to be *this* guy. Mom wasn't too crazy about him either, and one spring evening in a park as they sat and talked on a picnic blanket she told him it was over. This didn't sit well with him. He began to curse her and, filled with rage, held her down and began choking her. He was strong and fit but somehow my spunky little mother was able to get him off her and run. She ran scream-praying ("Hellllllp me, sweet Jesus—strengthen my legs! God above, save me now!") through the park to the main road and, miraculously, he was never able to catch up to her.

She hailed a passing car and without waiting yanked a door open and jumped in. A shocked but understanding couple drove her straight home. She woke us up and told us we were moving the next day. She wasn't sure where, but it was time to go and the "good Lord would provide." She called the men from the church for help.

That next morning one of them rented a U-Haul and helped us load everything up. His parents lived out in Utah, and he suggested that out West would be a good place to start over: a clean and friendly environment where we could distance ourselves from the kooks Mom had been dating. Another kind man showed up with his comfortable new Ford LTD. We left our 1971 Volkswagen Beetle behind, knowing full well that it stood no chance of crossing the Great Plains, as it could barely make it to the A&P without suffering seizures and spasms befitting a poisoning victim. We piled into the spacious Ford and the cab of the U-Haul. Both men took time off from their jobs and, leaving their families for a week, drove us 1,900 miles west.

I don't recall either of those two saintly men being charming or having bigger-than-life personalities. Neither was terribly flashy or slick. In fact, both of them seemed a little on the quiet, humble side. But their selfless actions reflected their genuine concern for us. They cared.

In Utah there was no lack of people reaching out to offer assistance or service to a single mom with a full load. Once again other men became role models for me, mostly my friends' dads, who were patient and accepting. Most were hard-working, honest men who cared for their own and extended kindnesses to others. Still, I never felt entirely comfortable with kids who had both a mom and dad at home, especially if the dad made a decent living. Somehow I felt inferior to these kids and unworthy of their friendship, feelings my sweet mother exorcised with positive and uplifting words of encouragement. And she mostly succeeded.

I remember one girl I really liked told me her dad made $32,000 a year! (This was 1979, mind you—and Utah, to boot!) I was crushed. I knew I could never be with her. We were in totally different worlds—a princess and a pauper, separated by the chasm of disparate incomes. Hers was the kind of home where they could buy two or three gallons of milk *at the same time*! My mom would buy one half gallon and mix it with powdered milk and water in an empty gallon jug. I had serious doubts that any member of this girl's family had ever, out of absurd necessity, used newspaper, grocery bags or hand towels as a substitute for toilet paper like we did. Her family drove a beautiful blue Chevy Suburban, with automatic transmission, leather seats and air conditioning; we had a mud brown Chevy Nova, with a "three on the tree" tranny, plastic seats and squeaky-stiff roll-down windows. I reasoned that anybody whose dad could pull up to a gas station and *fill the tank* instead of just putting in whatever they had dug from their purse or car ashtray ($3.86 or $7.04) was as likely to be my girlfriend as I was likely to ever let her see, much less step foot in, our rental unit. (It would be years before I finally allowed a girl to visit me at home, and that was in college, when you were expected to live in squalor without suffering any dings to your pride.)

It Takes a Thief

And so, due to my social insecurity, I made close friends with boys whose parents were divorced or had economic circumstances that more closely matched my own. We had a bond: we were all pretty poor . . . and so we stole. Once we got past the initial conscience-rending guilt of stealing (sadly, it didn't take us long), we hardened our hearts and embraced the ease of breaching society's trust. Sure, many decent people would offer us summer work in their cherry or apple orchards, mowing lawns or chopping wood to try to teach us hard work and self-sufficiency, but we rarely lasted more than a day or two on the job before we reckoned stealing what we wanted was easier. We'd rather have been sneaking in to see *Star Wars* or *Smokey and the Bandit* on a hot summer day than balancing for our lives on top of a rickety wooden ladder leaning against the bough of a cherry tree and filling our buckets for 25¢ a crate.

Well-intentioned adults would pay us up front to deliver the *Shopper's Guide,* a free weekly newspaper, to a hundred or so doorsteps. We'd take the cash and dump the papers in a garbage bin. We needed money to play all those arcade games and foosball, and my friends knew where their older siblings hid their savings. And if we were out of quarters, we knew where to get slugs or how to use static electricity to shock the games and get free credits.

When we were hungry we'd go to the supermarket and eat right off the shelves. We'd walk into restaurants and ask to use the bathroom. On our way out of the restaurant, we'd split up and steal the tips left on the tables. On Labor Day weekend we'd use fake names and sign up at 7-Eleven to take around milk cartons to collect donations for the Jerry Lewis Telethon and then keep the money (I didn't care for that scheme too much; in fact, often my conscience would rear its long-dormant head and poke at me from somewhere deep down).

At some point we upped the ante and began stealing out of cars. Then homes. Anything people left in plain sight was fair game. We stole from lockers at the city pool. We stole from school. We stole from church (curiously, and I would say significantly, we never stole a dime from offerings we were assigned to collect from church members). We stole from people who went to church, *while they were at church.* Our neighbors. Our friends. We stole from the very men who reached out to us in love and patience.

We were lazy, ungrateful, disrespectful and shameless. We were bad kids, but we didn't have "hearts of gold." Not unless we ripped them off from someone else. What made matters infinitely worse was we were truant. We were wreaking much of this havoc *during school.* My dear mother, to be able to better provide for our teenager needs like food, food and more food (and Clearasil and terry cloth polo shirts), eventually caved and took a job that required her to leave the house each day at 7 a.m. She trusted that I was getting myself up, getting ready and getting to school; being responsible—a good young man.

I did, nor was, none of those things.

I was in seventh grade. I was sleeping in until nine or ten or whenever *The Price Is Right* came on. I'd lie around watching TV until my friends came over and it was time to go out and find something illegal to do. In a single term of forty-five school days, I was absent thirty-eight of them.

CHAPTER ONE

My grade point average was a negative integer. I'd intercept phone calls and messages from the school.

And then I got caught.

We all did, really. We weren't exactly criminal masterminds; we were just felonious juveniles living on the edge. One Sunday afternoon we skipped out of church services early to raid the faithful's homes—as was our custom. While climbing into a neighbor's home through a back window in broad daylight, my friend Casey suddenly stopped halfway in. From where Eric, our other accomplice, and I were standing we saw nothing, but we could hear a female voice. The wonderful mother of the home, Mrs. Fielding, was sitting in a chair right by the window. The curtains were closed, so we hadn't seen her. Without skipping a beat, Casey—as nonchalantly as he could sound on all fours climbing through the window, his rear end pointing back out at us—pleasantly said, "Oh, hi. Is Curtis [her son] home?"

At this point, Eric and I would have been smart to turn tail and run. This was Casey's problem now. There's no honor among thieves. So long, sucker. But, ever the actor, I felt compelled to corroborate Casey's brilliant cover ploy and piped up, "What time *is* it anyway? Is Curtis at church?" Mrs. Fielding pulled the curtains back and saw Eric and me. She didn't have the usual warm smile that was typical of her. She looked disappointed.

"Oh, hello, Mrs. Fielding. How are you?" I continued the charade. "Is it time for church already?"

She said nothing. She looked unhappy, but not angry.

"Daylight savings," Eric contributed. "That's right. It's an hour later than what we thought. Shoot." He was good.

"I guess we'd better get over to the church, then," I said. "Great to see you. Please tell Curtis we said 'Hi.' Oh, wait, I guess we'll just tell him ourselves over there. Ha ha."

Casey slowly backed out and dropped down to the ground. We took off, thinking we were in the clear, giggling to shake off the nervous rush we felt. Rather than cut our losses and race back to church, we actually had the audacity to move on to the next house, where we found $33 in cash in the bureau of the master bedroom. We took it and buried it under a rock in a field near my apartment and then headed back to the chapel to be there when the meetings ended, innocent as can be.

The very next morning my new life as a former criminal began.

My mother entered my room to wake me up at 7 a.m. She had that look on her face that shot terror through me from my head to my toes, and I knew that she knew about everything—about stealing, about school, about lying to her; that look only a mother can authentically muster that simultaneously registers shock, anger and deep hurt.

Before we were taken into police custody to be booked, the officers agreed to hold a sort of informal court for the benefit of the adult neighbors. The detective assigned to investigate the rash of burglaries and thefts in the area was keen to hear our full confessions, as were our parents and the other adult victims. They gathered, some twenty or so, in the front room of the Fielding's home. Every schoolkid, friend or foe, within two miles was waiting on the front lawn while the closed-door testimonials took place. Each of us, five in total, took our turns one by one spilling our guts and baring our souls to the gallery.

The shame I felt was indescribable. We had hurt people. Lost their trust. Caused them grief and trouble. We had disrespected them and victimized them. Entered their homes, violated their privacy and their property. We had no excuses for our actions. We knew what we were doing was wrong. We chose to break the law. We wanted money and we didn't want to work for it.

After several hours of painful testimony, and to my eternal horror, we were frisked, handcuffed and paraded out the front door past all the other noncriminal kids (later my mother told me that the police didn't actually require any of the showy displays of collaring us like hardened criminals on the lam, but our parents had insisted so that we felt the full impact of our actions). We were fingerprinted, arrested and put in a holding cell for many hours before being released to go home with our parents.

The months leading up to my court appearance before a juvenile judge were the most agonizing imaginable. I did everything in my power to change my ways, to mend my errors, to pay back my debts (we recovered the money under the rock and gave it back) and to try to erase the look of sadness and embarrassment in my mother's eyes. I confessed everything to the judge and bawled my eyes out. It required no acting talent at all; I was sincerely remorseful. I was ready to mow His Honor's lawns, take out His Honor's garbage and massage His Honor's smelly feet for a year to stay out of a juvenile facility. Fortunately, that wasn't necessary. He put me on probation for six months and ordered restitution.

But the most lasting memory is how the people forgave us. And I don't just mean those who were offended by our brazen lawlessness and the shame we brought upon the neighborhood and its good reputation, but most importantly those from whom we stole: our victims. These people were amazing. They didn't stop reaching out to see how they could help my family. The good men and women of the church and neighborhood still took an interest in helping me learn life skills, have appropriate fun and reconstruct my hardened heart. It seemed, even more than before, they cared about me.

And there's the point (finally!). In spite of everything awful that I'd done, every obvious and justifiable reason they had to shun me and give up on me as a lost cause, they just kept caring. They were genuinely concerned to see me succeed. I suspect much of their concern was based more on their love and respect for my mother, whom most held in the highest esteem. She was positive, optimistic, outgoing and hardworking. An inspiration, really. But they forgave me and didn't look back.

In fact, one of the men from whom I'd stolen was handy with electronics. For Christmas that year Mom had saved up enough to get me a tape recorder from Radio Shack. Given my shameless behavior over the previous few months, I couldn't believe how fortunate I was to have received such an amazing present. Fittingly, it turned out to be about as amazing as you would expect a Tandy Radio Shack electronic device to be, and it quickly went on the fritz. My mother strongly suggested I call this kind gentleman to ask if he could help me fix it. I felt sure he was still very upset with me and I didn't dare. She made me call him anyway. He invited me to come over to his home, where I sat with him in his little workshop and he carefully took apart my cherished Christmas gift. He spoke to me kindly. There was no judgment or frustration in his tone. He asked about my interests, hobbies (the new, legal ones) and what I wanted to be someday. We had a sweet conversation as he generously fixed my tape recorder. He never once even mentioned what I had done, much less availed himself of the opportunity to chew me out.

For as humble, quiet and calm as this man was, it would be impossible for me to categorize him as anything *but* a *People* Person.

A few years later another genuinely caring family, the Millers, took me in for a summer while Mom was back in Michigan visiting her mother and siblings. Though the Millers were far better off financially than anyone I had met until then, and of another faith than my own, they made me feel as comfortable as if I were at home (except *their* home had a swimming pool, new cars and limitless rolls of cushiony, two-ply toilet paper!). They were unpretentious, authentic and fun, like my family. They had two sons, Todd and Matt, who were both about my age. We all enjoyed the same playful and somewhat irreverent sense of humor. Mr. Miller amazed me with his piano skills. He played by ear and could conjure up pretty much any tune we requested. Mrs. Miller was a wonderful mother, requiring each of us to perform daily house chores (just like my mom) before allowing—and encouraging—us to enjoy the summer days of our youth playing in the pool or chasing girls. Often simultaneously.

They opened their home to me, together with all the attendant niceties they gave to their own sons—money for this or that, summer movies, keys to the cars and a comfortable bed. My mom didn't pay them to put me up. She offered, of course, but they refused reimbursement; they understood our situation and were happy to welcome me.

These people, like so many others that influenced me in my youth, stand out in my memory as examples of real People People. They weren't necessarily outgoing, gregarious and transparent, but a few were. They didn't regularly go out of their way to socialize with strangers or grow their ever-expanding circle of friends, but some would. A few of them were even flat-out shy and reserved.

But every one of them, in their own way, was happy and successful.

For many years I have admired and appreciated People People for the impact they have had on my personal and professional life. I have carefully observed certain character traits, attitudes and actions that People People share. This book is about discovering how to become more like them, especially as adults at work, who likely make up a majority of readers. Subsequently, it won't be too difficult to apply the principles learned here in your personal life as well. If you're at all like me, you'll quickly identify how far short you fall stacked up to a real People Person, but with a simple game plan plus a dump truck of medication and a decade of therapy you'll probably improve some.

CHAPTER TWO
What Is a People Person and Why Should I CARE? Part One

On a mid-January Saturday afternoon in San Francisco, Vernon Leonard Davis, 6 feet 3 inches and 250 pounds of ripped, lean muscle, wrapped his massive arms around his boss in a bear hug and bawled on his shoulder like a baby in front of millions of people watching on live television.

With only eight seconds left on the clock and the San Francisco 49ers comeback season on the brink of terminating, Davis had just caught the winning pass from quarterback Alex Smith. A first-round draft pick in 2006, Davis was the highest paid tight end in league history at the time, but it took three seasons of injuries and mediocre performances before Davis finally started to exhibit hints of his much-hyped potential. Still, under the guidance of Mike Singletary, a serious and stern coach who offered little in the way of praise and kindness to his players, especially to Davis, the team won only eight games in 2009 and only six in 2010.

Then the organization made a significant change. They spent millions to lure Jim Harbaugh away from Stanford University to come coach the woeful 49ers. Harbaugh was considered by many to be a gamble. Still relatively new to head coaching, he had only delivered two winning seasons at Stanford and was known as much for his unconventional "people" approach to coaching players as for his NFL career as a quarterback. A few players were swapped out for others, but the core of the underachieving team remained. In 2011, under Harbaugh's guidance, San Francisco broke its decade-long slump and won fourteen games, including the heart-stopping playoff match against the New Orleans Saints.

From six wins to fourteen in a single year—what made the difference? The team more than doubled its victories without major player changes. How?

There's a reason Coach Harbaugh was the first person Davis went to on the sidelines and embraced. He trusted him. Davis knew that he could safely wrap his coach in a bear hug and weep on his shoulder without fear of rejection or humiliation. Harbaugh personified a massive overhaul in the culture of the program, a new atmosphere that cornerback Carlos Rogers credited as one of the main reasons for his own successes on the field (six interceptions in 2011–12). Harbaugh was a head coach who truly cared about his players as people, a competent football strategist who also recognized the silliness and joy of grown husbands and fathers playing a kids' game for millions of dollars.

"It's fun. He's a little crazy," said Rogers. "You'll see the guy holding field goals for [the kicker], taking snaps at quarterback, throwing the ball to the receivers when they're going over their routes . . . talking to DBs . . . just having fun throughout the whole practice. He has fun and he interacts with every position."[1]

Here was a coach that treated his players like people and not merely chess pieces and, significantly, encouraged fun. The kickoff team danced to upbeat music just before each kick. Opposing teams tried to stare them down with serious, manly growls and glares, but the Niners' players just kept on bouncing, grooving and loosening themselves up with their playful, crowd-pleasing dancing. In postgame speeches Harbaugh was effusive and specific with his praise and love for his players. His calling guys out for the good things they did earned him far more respect than berating them for missing a tackle or blowing an assignment. At the end of every postgame speech, the team huddled up as Harbaugh shouted, "Whooooooo's got it better than *us*?" In unison the entire team, including assistant coaches, trainers and any other employee of the 49ers organization present responded, "Noooooooo-*body*!"

But don't misunderstand. Harbaugh successfully mixed that personable, fun spirit with hard work. "Long practices, long meetings," Rogers said. "We [were] there from I guess eight in the morning 'til probably eight at night."[2]

As with any high-profile job, Harbaugh had his share of critics. Many believed that his soft approach to leadership would have a short shelf life in the high-pressure arena of professional football. But Harbaugh's authentic approach to coaching has served his teams well, so far.

"They absolutely love the guy [Harbaugh]," a TV announcer said as Harbaugh hugged the sobbing Davis. "That's why they play so hard for him."

This book is not so much about defining what makes a People Person, but instead about *redefining* it. Or better put, adding to it. I decided a long time ago that the commonly held view of People People— outgoing, social and comfortable among the species—was severely lacking. It also had a certain ambiguity to it. Hard to define, and not quickly understood. "We hired a new CEO who's a real '*people* person,' ya know? Things are totally different around here now." I've heard something like this dozens of times and I'm confident that in every case the speaker had a different reason for describing their new CEO as a People Person. Is the new CEO outgoing and likable? Or does she have compassion for people? Or both?

A People Person is so much more than just someone who can hold their own at a social gathering or successfully host a team of potential business clients from China over an entire weekend. That describes the most traditional type of People Person, a Type I.

Type I People People

A Type I People Person (T1) is someone who can smoothly engage in effective, pleasant human interactions. T1s are completely comfortable around other humans, even total strangers, with whom they seem to always want to connect. They aim to please. They are cheerful, engaging and outgoing. In a group setting, classroom or auditorium they'll sit right up front or in the middle of others. A T1 greets others, remembers their names and asks about family members. They want—even need—to be around other humans and interact with them. Most Type I People People are excellent at networking.

You've likely heard a Type I described like this: "Oh, that Hortense; she's a real *people* person. You're going to *love* her!" Or possibly: "His success doesn't surprise me at all, because Flabio's a real *people* person." If you're like me (after first quietly snickering at the names Hortense and Flabio) you probably assessed the comment, nodded in agreement and thought, "You know, we could *use* more people like that around here."

And you'd be right. Type I People People are somewhat rare, because in many cases they come by it naturally. Like a special, inherited gift. It is who they are, either due to environmental conditions in their childhood or because they were just born that way. They add variety and spice to whatever environment they're in. There seems to be more jocularity and levity when a T1 is around. The assets that T1s possess can, of course, be learned, and myriad are the converted to their ranks.

Many of us, and I include myself in this group, are less naturally inclined to make seeking out human contact as persistent a practice as a T1. For any number of reasons, it requires *effort* for us to exhibit Type I traits. We occasionally enjoy spontaneous conversations with strangers or dining with clients or prospects, but we can also happily go lengthy stretches *without* collaborating, connecting or conversing. Our packed rush-hour freeways are evidence of our preference for solitude, as carpools and buses filled with T1s zip by in the commuter lane while the rest of us loners stop and start in bumper-to-bumper traffic. We like and need our time in the car alone. *We* select the song or talk station and set the volume that best suits *our* mood. Sometimes we talk out loud to ourselves, or to the man upstairs.

This self-selected seclusion does not make us any less gifted than Type I People People; our people strengths simply lie in other areas. We may not be as personable or social, either because we choose not to be or because we don't know how, but we can *learn* to be those things, and it would serve us well to do so. Especially as our Jetsons, space-age, hi-tech society makes connecting with people more challenging day by day.

Consider the following totally plausible scenario with a wholly fictional character not at all meant to resemble anyone living, dead or from a Twilight novel:

> Byron Van Mangents starts his day by throwing on a robe or a pair of shorts to go in search of the newspaper somewhere on, in or around his driveway. He grumbles to himself about the "good old days" when a paperboy made sure the paper was delivered right on his doorstep, where Byron could crack the door open in his underwear, reach down and safely pull the paper inside. The deliverer, probably a kid named Corky, knew that this kind of service would insure a nice tip when he came around to Byron's house each month to collect subscription fees. Byron himself had a paper route when he was a boy and remembered the dreaded collecting chores. He was only ten or eleven years old, out knocking on dozens of neighbors' doors, making his rounds, engaging customers in conversation and handling checks, cash and sometimes extending credit to those who were strapped. "I'll catch you next month, okay?" they'd tell him. No such interaction even remotely exists now. Once or twice in the past few years Byron has

been up early enough to see the anonymous adult delivery person hurl the newspaper from their car window like a ransom note taped to a rock and speed away to the next customer's home three blocks away. *Read it online,* they must be thinking, *you're really inconveniencing me here!* Of course Byron will eventually check updated news online and other information throughout the workday, but he still likes the feel of reading printed words.

Two days a week Byron telecommutes from the comfort of his home office. He spends the entire workday in his sky blue boxer briefs and Styx *Mr. Roboto* World Tour concert tee, and rarely communicates with anyone beyond a handful of e-mails.

But today is an "office" day. On his way to work, Byron stops for gas at the self-serve island, where he dispenses the fuel himself and pays at the pump. He listens to a little music on the radio, which is programmed and broadcast by computer. There is no live DJ, just an occasional recorded voice track naming the song and artist. Byron is cost conscious and green so he parks his car in the commuter lot and takes the bus to work. He self-scans his bus pass without a look at the driver. He and the other seventeen passengers pop in their earbuds and tune in to their music, audio books or podcasts. Some are busy on their iPads, others rapidly sending off texts, still others are playing video games or watching season three of *Blossom.*

At work, Byron uses his employee badge to securely enter the facility, walking past the long-retired security booth. Once snugly in his office cocoon, he begins his work behind a computer screen, writing code, answering e-mails and texts and occasionally chatting with coworkers and friends on Facebook or Windows Live until lunch. He brought his lunch from home and eats at his desk, where he can catch up on the news of the day, funny YouTube links sent to him by others and an episode of *Swamp People* on Netflix. After work he stops off at the library to check out an audio book through the self-checkout kiosk. He also buys a few necessary items from the grocery store using the automated checkstand. Just outside the grocery store is a Redbox kiosk. He pauses to scroll through the new releases, then decides to go to the Cineplex instead. At the movie theater, Byron avoids the lines of people and uses the automated ticket machine to select his movie and buy his ticket.

Once home, after checking his voice messages, e-mails and Facebook messages, Byron drops into bed, realizing he has completed an eighteen-hour day without interacting with a single human being face to face.

In this increasingly complicated and competitive world, developing and consistently exhibiting Type I behaviors is a challenge. As technology evolves at blinding speed and gradually sedates the masses by simplifying and automating daily routines, allowing people to hide behind their monitors, avatars and usernames, Type I People People would prefer torture such as waterboarding or a Tyler Perry movie over losing touch with humanity. When given the choice, they prefer a phone call to a text. A face-to-face chat over an e-mail. A handshake and a grin over an emoticon.

Type I People People are anxious to get to parties or social events where they can meet and connect with real live people. They engage in friendly, trivial conversations with people in line at the grocery store because they genuinely enjoy the interaction. If they could, they would pick up a hitchhiker every single day on their way to work just to have a total stranger to talk to and learn about. (You don't see a lot of hitchhikers anymore, do you? Most are probably on death row, you know, because they're all psychopathic killers!) T1s love the idea of sharing a cab with a total stranger; I'm not even a fan of sharing one with *people I know*. ("How do we split the fare?" "Who's paying the tip?" "Why is your knee almost touching mine?")

T1s have firm handshakes and look you in the eye when they speak. They don't stand too close to you, but not too far away either. They aren't uncomfortable giving hugs or kisses in greetings or goodbyes. They aren't shy or nervous addressing an audience. In fact, they are good public communicators; from the boardroom to the auditorium they can do razzle-dazzle or straight talk, and they're loud, proud and good with the crowd. They smile, wink, wave and say "hello" to neighbors, coworkers and passersby. They're cheerful and sometimes even, yes, bubbly. Their outwardly positive gestures and kind, polite words actually serve to brighten others' moods and constitute a form of service to those around them.

Big question: Why? Why do T1s act the way they do?

Answer: I don't know. I am not a social scientist, biologist, physician, geneticist or even very smart at all. My intent is to help others identify some fairly obvious differences between themselves and people that, to me at least (and I am the one writing the book here), seem to enjoy a higher level of satisfaction, joy and reward in their professional and personal lives.

I have determined this about T1s, however: their motives, conscious or not, can potentially be more selfish than altruistic. Altruism is defined as "the intention to benefit others at a cost to oneself." Selfishness is mostly the opposite: the intent to benefit oneself, and often it's at a cost to others. In the workplace, as in other group settings, there is a positive, significant status or prestige associated with altruists. Even though there is a cost, altruism indeed has its eventual rewards—respect from peers, power, affection from others, wider influence, trust, etc.—that ultimately allow the altruist to recoup the initial costs of their selflessness, and in some cases to wildly profit. The return on altruism can in fact be so bountiful that researchers have recently identified the contradictory term "competitive altruism" as a regular occurrence among humans. It is exactly what it sounds like: individuals performing altruistic deeds or being generous to the point of pain in an attempt to gain more long-term rewards. In other words, selflessness for selfish reasons.[3]

Thus it may be helpful to think of Type I People People as "style over substance," which doesn't necessarily mean T1s are shallow or superficial, but simply that the People People qualities they possess are mostly outward expressions and may not be genuinely motivated or an honest reflection of who they really are.

Type II People People

Type II People People (T2s) are "substance over style." They genuinely *care* about people, regardless of their desires or need to be with people or a complete lack of sociality. Their altruism is genuinely motivated and based on doing the right thing, and not "what's in this for me?"

T2s, by definition, do not possess all of the traditional extrovert attributes of T1s. For example, a T2 may not be up for a Friday night ball game with a bunch of coworkers, but he'll go anyway because his friends really want him to. A T2 might actually prefer an evening or a whole weekend with the phone off the hook and no one around but the dog, to read a book or go camping alone. But if someone needs her she'll set it all aside and help out.

Type II People People listen carefully and don't judge. They don't insinuate, beat around the bush or blow smoke. They tell it like it is.

They take your word for it. And when they give you theirs, they honor it.

They give credit where it's due and recognize effort.

If they're serving as leaders, they lead by example and open, honest communication. If they're serving as followers, they follow enthusiastically.

They are confident but not cocky. They're sincere, but carefully so.

They're happy for you when you succeed, and try to share your joys, pains, triumphs and failures.

They may not be comfortable initiating a hug or kiss as a greeting, but are willing to reciprocate in kind.

Type II People People enjoy the ride, bumpy or smooth. Their day-to-day optimism, seasoned with frivolity and laughter, is a deliberate choice they make, not the fortunate result of a charmed life devoid of pain, woes and afflictions. Type II People People nurture that prized possession of perspective.

At work, T2s "get it." They know that the burden of being a great place to work or having an attractive culture doesn't solely rest on the shoulders of the organization or its senior leaders. A Type II People Person knows that a strong, engaging work environment is not just the automatic outcome of well-designed and often expensive programs, perks and "people first" promises. That special spirit that permeates truly engaging workplaces is a product of individual commitment. It's what each person contributes daily that defines and reinforces culture; not the last rah-rah speech delivered by the CEO or the generous 401(k) matching. A Type II gets that.

When a company's leadership team identifies "People First," for example, as its slogan and stresses it as the foundational value of the company, Type IIs understand that it will require individuals to actually *live* a people-first philosophy among their coworkers and clients, and not merely point to new company perks or programs as evidence of a caring culture.

Type II People People give the benefit of the doubt and are quick to let offenses go. They are genuinely proud of others' successes and encourage them. They really *do* put *people first.*

In short, Type II is the next order of People People. It is the higher law of humanity.

To be clear, a Type II can thrive among humans without having Type I qualities, though there are normally some overlaps that naturally occur. For example, a public speaker that truly *cares about her audience*

(Type II) would naturally choose to deliver a presentation that is *engaging, humorous or compelling* in some way (Type I). A supervisor that is committed to *sincerely recognizing* his employee's best efforts (Type II) will need to *connect* with those employees, observe their behaviors and eventually *communicate publicly* his appreciation (Type I). A wise Type II will continually seek opportunities to perfect her Type I skills as she recognizes their value in forming caring relationships with others.

The opposite is even more important for T1s, since they have difficulty truly progressing as people without developing and internalizing T2 traits. *Smiles, pats on the back, pumping handshakes and bear hugs* (Type I) quickly run their course and are perceived as merely superficial devices if they aren't extensions of *genuine affection for people* (Type II). Even sincere attempts to *strike up conversations with strangers* (Type I) or *make new friends at work* will eventually fall short if they are only motivated by increasing one's own personal influence and exposure, building out a network or meeting one's selfish need to hear one's own voice. An *extroverted nature and zero fear of swag-seeking trade show attendees* may serve you well in wrangling prospects into your booth (Type I), but without a *genuine concern for their actual business needs* (Type II) or answering their legitimate questions, those attendees' stay in your booth will be brief. They may pretend to listen long enough to earn the free stuffed armadillo company mascot for their nephew, but not a second longer.

TYPE III People People

When T1s have truly developed T2 concern for others and when T2s finally master T1 skills—and for most this is a lifelong journey—the zenith of the People People quest has been achieved: the Type III (T3). It is to this lofty summit humans should aspire. The permanent union of social skills *and* people-first principles is the eventual goal. It is indeed rare air; lofty stuff. These are true People People. Of course they continue to progress, improve, hone, sharpen and perfect. But don't read any more into it than what's been written. Attaining T3 status need not be equated with an eternal quest to approach divinity. There are indeed other, more specific paths that lead to that outcome. People People need not adhere to any particular set of tenets or beliefs. The atheist. The agnostic. The believer. All can become People People. Most will find it a struggle and a stretch to authentically meld T1 and T2 values. For others it seems to come easier.

A limo driver named Leonard Greene greeted me near baggage claim at Orlando International not long ago. The company that had invited me to come speak at their employee meetings, Express Employment, had sent the car and driver to pick me up; otherwise, believe me, I would have rented from Avis, as is my longtime habit. I'm not a limo guy by nature, but after a long flight I certainly wasn't begrudging the chance to chill out in a comfy car.

Leonard greeted me with a warm, full, toothy smile. He reminded me a lot of a younger Denzel Washington, who, for my money, is still one of the most watchable screen presences today. But I digress (get used to it). Since age twelve, Leonard, now forty-three, had had "hundreds of jobs," but loved driving best because it gave him "the daily opportunity to meet new people and help them." In fact, he said it was this "*need* to be with *and* serve others" that made it difficult to stay with one job too long.

"I like working with people. I get the best satisfaction out of other people being satisfied," Leonard said. "I was doing firefighting, for instance, which I loved, but you didn't interact with people as much. And when you did, it was like you were a hero. I'd prefer to be less of a hero and just *be* with people more. That's why I love this job."

Leonard goes the extra mile to satisfy his passengers. He bought a tackle box from Walmart and fills each slot with a different brand of gum, candy or breath mint to offer his clients. Before the airport banned the practice (for security purposes—ha!), Leonard would occasionally bring his own red carpet to roll out from the passenger door of his town car.

When he found out he had executives from Pepsi flying in, he brought some Pepsi signs and posters from home (he worked for Pepsi once, naturally) and adorned the inside of the vehicle.

He is friendly, outgoing, happy and eager to talk. In our twenty or so minutes together, this point he made jumped out at me: "A lot of drivers just drive for a living. It's just a job to them. Some do nice things for people or smile and talk, but it's not always real. They do it for the tip or repeat business. Their motives are different than mine. I do it because I have a need to connect with people. I have to fulfill it. If I was [alone] on an island, I'd never make it." Leonard laughed. "I'd kill myself."

It's interesting to note that Leonard differentiates his motives from those of other drivers doing nice things for people. Some do it for the tip, but Leonard says he does it because *he "needs" to.* Fundamentally both of these motives are selfish. They both serve the server, even though Leonard's reasons *seem* more altruistic.

But after digging deeper I discovered more Type II motives. Leonard recalled that his favorite job was working at a Marriott Hotel in the Florida Keys: "I started in the kitchens, coming in at 3 a.m. to set up the breakfast buffets, but of course I wanted to do something with people. I would occasionally help out people here and there, but I wanted more." Because of his extroverted personality, huge smile and eagerness to help guests, he was promoted to work at the front desk. "I loved it," Leonard said. "I love solving problems for people. Answering the phones and handling their problems."

Leonard admitted that working with people was "like a drug. I have to have it." Again, some Type I People People are extroverted and amiable because it's good for *them.* But Leonard went beyond the T1 craving to interact with others *and* having the T1 people skills to do it; he was also passionate about *helping others* and he truly *cared* about people, both T2 traits. By my own definition, in Leonard Greene I had met a Type III People Person. He was outgoing, jovial, friendly and well spoken, but was motivated by concern for other people, even total strangers.

When Leonard received handsome tips, referrals and repeat business, it was not the expected product of a carefully designed "If A (hustle, smile, serve), then B ($$$)" strategy; it was the rewarding outcome for providing genuine, personable service with a real smile and no expectation of additional benefits.

Everyone Else: The Unenlightened and Aspirants

This category includes those who do not identify with People People of any type. They have no appreciable people skills (T1) and don't put people first (T2), which isn't to say that they don't care about other people. They are not against becoming People People; they are neutral to positive. Many are simply ignorant of the People People concept: the Unenlightened. Others are Aspirants, People People in embryo. This is a huge group of people, probably including many of your coworkers and neighbors, and this book will help open their eyes. In fact, you should probably buy several copies for your coworkers and neighbors.

Jerks

Like Everyone Else, Jerks are *neither* T1s nor T2s, but unlike Everyone Else, Jerks are negative. In other words, they have no social skills, tact, grace, communication skills (Type I) *and* don't really care about people at all (Type II). They are the opposite of T3s.

A few words of caution: T1s can sometimes be confused with Jerks. For this reason it is critical for T1s to begin developing T2 traits. And Jerks can temporarily fake both T1 and T2 behaviors. But T2s are rarely Jerk-like, nor do they permanently possess any Jerk traits. They certainly are not perfect. They often make rash choices and embarrassing errors, but a Type II People Person avoids Jerkiness at all costs; that's what makes him or her a Type II.

A Type I, on the other hand, walks a fine line, because in spite of a total lack of Jerk-like intentions, an exclusive Type I People Person lacks the Type II foundation she needs to prevent herself from exhibiting Jerk behaviors or, worse, completely crossing over to the Jerk side.

To summarize:

Type I People People may or may not be good people; however they are always good *with* people. Most mean well but lack the depth of sincerity that adopting Type II traits would provide them. To fully thrive among humans, all T1s must eventually adopt T2 values or run the risk of becoming Jerks.

Type II People People are usually good people. They may not be good *with* people, but they are usually good *to* people. Ideally they try to incorporate Type I characteristics into their personality (like being good with people), but can survive with limited Type I traits. Successful adoption of T1 traits (becoming a T3) should be their ultimate goal.

Type III People People are good *with* people *and* good *to* people. They *are* People People. In algebraic terms that even the most simian mind can compute:

T1 + T2 = T3 (a true People Person)

Everyone Else (the Unenlightened and Aspirants) is exactly that, except for Jerks. This is a category of people for whom this book might make an excellent birthday present.

Jerks are not People People. Jerks can and will fake certain People People traits, but they are eventually exposed as rude, tactless and uncaring. This doesn't mean that anyone who is not a People Person is automatically a Jerk; they may simply be in the Everyone Else classification.

It is typically at this juncture in my speeches or workshops when the question is raised, "Don't 'nice guys' finish last?" This is often followed by its first cousin: "There sure are a lot of Jerks out there doing pretty well for themselves!"

Nice Guys and Jerks

A study published in the journal *Social Psychological and Personality Science* concluded that people who break the rules, flaunt societal norms or act rudely (i.e., Jerks) are perceived as more powerful than their more civil counterparts. When people have power—either formal or informal, depending on their title, position, resources or politics—they act the part. Powerful people smile less, interrupt others and speak in a louder voice. Curiously, the study found that even people *without* power, but who don't respect the basic rules of social behavior, actually lead others to believe that they *do* have power.

The Jerk-esque examples used in the research included a traveler ignoring an "Employees Only" sign near a coffeepot and boldly helping himself to a cup; a man behaving rudely at a restaurant—putting his feet up on a chair and flicking his cigarette ashes on the floor; a bookkeeper bending certain accounting rules as a shortcut; and a student arriving late, throwing his bag down and putting his feet up on the table. The rule breakers were perceived by observers as more in control and more powerful compared to people who didn't steal the coffee or didn't break accounting rules. Participants viewed these people as more likely to "get to make decisions" and able to "get people to listen to what [they say]." They are viewed as having a stronger will and greater sense of liberation to do what they please because they seem to have more power.[1]

What makes people rise to power has long been a question in social science. Previous research has found predictors of power such as personality traits like extroversion and dominance, or demographic characteristics like gender or ethnicity, or nonverbal behaviors. This study now adds "violating norms" to the list of predictors. In People People terms, Jerks gain power by violating norms and seemingly get ahead.

Great. So nice guys *do* finish last? Don't let it keep you up at nights. The logic is flawed. A rude person's perceived power is a product of Jerky behavior and ultimately nets them nothing. Continued rudeness and norm violations are sure to end ugly. Here's how the scientists explained it:

> *Because power leads to behavioral dis-inhibition, the powerful are more likely to violate norms. Doing so in turn leads other people to perceive them as powerful, as we have demonstrated. As individuals thus gain power, their behavior becomes even more liberated, possibly leading to more norm violations, and thus evoking a self-reinforcing process. This vicious cycle of norm violations and power affordance may play a role in the emergence and perpetuation of a multitude of undesirable social and organizational behaviors such as fraud, sexual harassment, and violence.*[2]

CHAPTER THREE

I believe the adage "What goes around comes around" is a fitting phrase here.

How often we see full-on rude, gasbag Jerks that fraudulently Type I their way into an organization, many times in a leadership position. I am reminded of a company I worked for years ago where this happened. They were looking to replace an outgoing manager with a new hire, rather than promote from within, to stimulate a sense of new blood and fresh ideas. This flawed and all-too-common practice usually fails more than it succeeds. The candidate blew into the building with an easy breeziness, charming the ladies and impressing the gents. His comfortable smile and affable spontaneity made other applicants forgettable. The team was taken by his quick and insightful answers, his instant connection to others and his playful sense of humor. He was experienced, smart and capable. Of course he was hired. (No, it wasn't me. But I'm flattered you thought so.)

In short order, this charming "People Person" that everyone swooned over switched off the façade and became a rude, belittling power player. It's nothing new; it happens all the time. The bait and switch. The minute the contract was signed and while the ink on the ID badge photo was still drying, the show was over. He began playing his Jerk card to the fullest and, true to the research, was perceived as a powerful person. His brusque, succinct orders or put-downs were often mixed with an unsettling wry grin, leaving everyone to wonder if he was only kidding. He was not. He was a Jerk, grinning because he was pleased to be fulfilling his life's mission of terrorizing innocent peers and subordinates. His rudeness-power cycle continued at an accelerated pace until it evolved into charges of abuse and sexual harassment leveled by his staff.

Jerks may enjoy their power and successes for a season, but in the long run People People, "nice guys" if you will, finish first, laugh last and laugh best.

Why "Nice" Is Best

1. **Jerks burn out.** Self-serving actions, insincerity, superficial back-patting and shallow, showy gregariousness all have a very short shelf life. Anything of real value at work or home is a long-term proposition that requires authentic business and personal relationships. Short-term successes or temporary victories are the rewards of Jerks and even many TIs, but People People try to nurture relationships that bear lasting results. A skilled Jerk might fool some for a while, but will eventually be discovered and will require serious rehabilitation and conversion to the light side, or implosion is inevitable.

2. **People People endure.** They enjoy much greater levels of job security, tenure and even longer lives. Studies show that some of the eldest of elders are "nice guys." "When I started working with centenarians, I thought we'd find that they survived so long in part because they were mean and ornery," researcher Nir Barzilai said. His pessimistic instincts were a bit off. "When we assessed the personalities of . . . 243 centenarians, we found qualities that clearly reflect a positive attitude towards life. Most were outgoing, optimistic and easygoing. They considered laughter an important part of life and had a large social network. They expressed emotions openly rather than bottling them up."[3] In other words, these old-timers were People People: positive, outgoing, optimistic, easygoing, laughers and open with emotions.

3. **Nice guys (and girls) aren't doormats and pushovers.** People People are not, by definition, wimpy. Just because some of them do not possess the outspoken manner or debate skills

of a Type I trial lawyer in open court does not mean they are weak or will submissively defer to a loudmouth, hothead or smooth talker. Sure, some Type IIs might not hold a listener's attention, but it doesn't mean they can't hold their own in a serious debate or discussion. Warren Buffett has a reputation of being a down-to-earth guy, despite being one of the wealthiest people in the world. He lives in the same home he bought years ago for $31,000. He answers his own phone and wears clothes off the rack. His philanthropic efforts are legendary and he plans to leave 99 percent of his wealth to charity. You don't become a billionaire by letting others walk all over you, but it doesn't require walking all over others. Using intellect, hard work and ambition, Buffett has proven that nice guys can finish first.

4. **Laughing all the way to the bank.** *Harvard Business Review* published a study that found that people with a sense of humor make more money and move up the corporate ladder faster than their peers. Humor is a hallmark of People People, but is also one of a handful of characteristics common to Jerks as well. A People Person's sense of humor will typically be appropriate to the time, place and audience, whereas a Jerk's sense of humor, by definition, will be obnoxious, arrogant, crass or demeaning. A case can be made for a handful of hurtful, derisive, vulgar comics that have made obscene amounts of money being obscene— George Carlin, Andrew Dice Clay, Chelsea Handler, to name a few—but these are professional entertainers who've found their niche, not supervisors in the Finance Department at IBM. By the way, the wealthiest humorists ever? Jerry Seinfeld, Jay Leno, David Letterman, George Lopez, Bill Cosby, Johnny Carson. All have been celebrated

for their "good guy" comedy images. Though Carson's professional success relied heavily on the ease with which he engaged thousands of celebrity guests night after night for thirty years on *The Tonight Show* (T1), off the air he was a notorious recluse. He preferred privacy and solitude over socializing and doing the "LA thing." He supported many charities with his wealth throughout his life (T2) and even left $156 million after his death to hospitals, clinics and other charities. T1 + T2 = T3.

5. **The happiness factor.** From a work perspective, the happiest people are those in jobs that serve, help, lift, inspire, teach, aid and heal other people. More on that later. People People are far more likely to be happy in their *personal* lives as well. Putting people first means placing others' comfort, pleasure and needs before one's own. Can anything be more truly gratifying than selfless service to someone else? A transcendent piece of wisdom teaches that when you're feeling blue the quickest path to joy is to forget yourself and do something for another person. Some call it karma, others the law of the harvest. You reap what you sow. People People that truly get it and put others' happiness first inevitably are happier themselves.

Chances are excellent that you know plenty of T1s, T2s and even a few T3s. You can probably rattle off a quick list of three or four within seconds. You bump into them each day at work, at play, at home, in the boardroom, in the game room or in the family room.

You may already be a People Person yourself. A champion of the cause. You'll find bits and pieces of yourself in the pages ahead. Case studies, stories and truths shared here will encourage you and validate your existing efforts. Maybe by now you've identified yourself as a Type I or Type II and are feeling the not-so-subtle invitation to start acquiring what you lack.

Perhaps you, like Everyone Else, are among the Unenlightened or an Aspirant; not a Jerk, just a People Person in embryo. Everyone has the innate capacity to become one (even prison guards and tax accountants), but maybe you just need a little guidance and convincing. Or possibly you've already convinced yourself and everyone else that you're "just *not* a People Person!" and have already scribbled the word "Hermit" on your mailbox in preparation for a life of solitude and online gaming.

If so, remember: People People are more likely to be respected, admired, complimented, trusted, appreciated, recognized, rewarded and promoted throughout their longer and happier lives than those who simply do not know how to coexist with other humans. In traveling this amazing planet I have met successful individuals and entire organizations that wholeheartedly and gratefully attribute their worldly successes to putting people first. Studies, surveys and research validate their instinctive assumptions.

But go ahead, seal yourself away in your private world of gadgets and virtual reality and meditate to Simon and Garfunkel's "I Am a Rock"— and you run the serious risk of underachieving in all facets of life.

The fact is, even with an abundance of tangible and intangible evidence to support the notion, many people simply don't care. Having a soft spot for humanity may not be to everyone's liking. An important People People attribute is tolerance and respect for opposing views and interests, and that includes letting Everyone Else and Jerks be who they are. It's their choice. Sure, they'll probably end up burning in Hell for eternity, but who are we to say what's best for them?

Besides, many of them simply suffer from ignorance. They haven't identified specific People People traits or learned how to apply them. Until now, no book has specifically and deliberately treated the subject, except maybe the Holy Bible, written for an ancient civilization that probably didn't even have dial-up. But complete ignorance of People People principles as an excuse is a tough sell. Every person with the capacity for reason and judgment sees these attributes in action every day and can connect the dots. "Boy, that Dirk sure is a charming cuss," they think to themselves. "There's something about him that people seem to respond to. I wonder if I could be that way?"

I've already mentioned a dozen or more of these People People traits, nearly all of which fall neatly into one of four main People People areas: Communication, Authenticity, Respect and Enjoyment. Rest assured I am very aware that these four words combine to make the acronym CARE. In fact it took a team of highly paid marketing geniuses seventy-six combined billable hours to generate this nugget. But it works.

Because when all is said and done and written about transparency, empathy, sociability, perspective and so on, the quickest answer is that People People genuinely *care*.

Corny? Sure. A little.

But doggone it, that's really what it all comes back to. A People Person really cares about other people.

So, game over, right? You've got it figured. No more reading is necessary. Close the book and pass it on to the next eager reader, maybe the nice lady seated next to you on the plane who has zero intention of yielding a millimeter of space on the arm rest. She could use the book, clearly.

But there's more.

More

For example, from the title alone you may have thought that a book called *People People* is a volume of stories and research about the professionals who comprise the field of human resources—in many contemporary organizations known as the "*People* Department." While it's true that much of what is written here is of great value and applicability in the HR sphere (including a few HR-specific comments in Chapter Ten), the concept of People People stretches far beyond human resources, sales, marketing and other traditional "people" groups of the modern workplace. Indeed, it should be obvious that the notion goes beyond even the confines of the high-rise corporate tower, the business park with the fancy name and duck pond, or the north wing of Building Q.

People People are everywhere. They are teachers, doctors, nurses, pilots, lawyers, plumbers, police officers, soldiers and scientists. They are stay-at-home moms and dads. They are housekeepers, waiters, operators and customer *care* representatives (there's that word again).

In 2012, *Forbes* published an article highlighting a list of the best-paying jobs for "people persons." Not surprisingly, in the referenced study by jobs expert Laurence Shatkin, Ph.D., a "people person" is described as someone who is good at working with others, empathizing, and teaching or persuading others to agree with them—what Shatkin described as "social skills." More specifically, Shatkin looked at all the jobs in the U.S. Department of Labor's Occupational Information Network that were labeled as requiring skills of persuasion, negotiation, social perceptiveness, instructing others, coordinating efforts and service orientation.[4] These, Shatkin determined, were the characteristics that best described People People, essentially mirroring the commonly held definition that People People are persuasive and perceptive communicators and are "good *with* people." This, of course, is true, but only paints a piece of the picture—that of a T1 People Person.

So the study could have been more accurately named "The 20 Best-Paying Jobs for T1s," if only the Ph.D. smarty-pants had thought to consult me on it first.

But hey, whatever.

Shatkin ranked the jobs by median annual earnings for full-time workers, based on 2010 wage data from the U.S. Bureau of Labor Statistics. Marketing manager is the top-paying job for T1s, with an annual median salary of $112,800. "Marketing managers have to understand how to relate to others, and they need the power of persuasion," said Shatkin.[5]

No doubt. Still, a marketing manager may be an expert in persuasion and coordinating efforts, but still be a shallow, selfish Jerk. Do you know any marketing managers that fit that description? I've met one or seventeen in my lifetime.

A lawyer (No. 2 on the list), especially a trial attorney, will likely have social skills up the wazoo, but can turn those on and off like a light switch. The remainder of his interactions, away from the courtroom, may be rude and impolite and the impetus for countless lawyer jokes. (How many lawyer jokes are there? Just three. All the rest are true stories.)

Sales managers (No. 3), general business managers (No. 4), operations managers (No. 5) and school administrators (No. 6) all require certain people-facing, communication and instructive *skills* (T1) that do not automatically qualify them as People People. Sales people and compliance officers also made the list, as well as occupational therapists, physician's aids, dental hygienists and social workers,[6] the latter four being service jobs that are more T2-focused.

The problem with putting much stock in a list like this is that it can discourage Aspirants into believing that the best they can ever hope to do by being a People Person is to become a marketing manager making $112,800 a year. Nice guys really do finish last, they might reason. First, $112K ain't chump change where I'm from, and second, "nice guys (and gals)" who make more than a "comfortable" living are everywhere in all professions and trades: IT specialists, plumbers, real estate agents, auto dealers, investment bankers, pro athletes, rock stars, movie stars and crooked politicians. Not all of them earn obscene money, or need to, to be successful and enjoy a happy life. But don't feel as though your opportunities for worldly prosperity are capped because you are a genuine People Person.

People People Are Everywhere

In the past two decades, as I've traipsed around the worldwide speaking and training circuit, I've met thousands of People People. They qualify in myriad ways, but most are outgoing, friendly, sincere, compassionate, empathetic, gregarious, funny, thoughtful, authentic and kind. To some, a People Person is a Type II—humble, gracious and unassuming; the "salt of the earth." To others, a People Person is nothing more than a Type I—social, confident, passionate and a "mover and shaker." (Put the two together and you get "salt shaker." Rim shot.)

But one thread is common to all People People, from the demure to the flamboyant. They see things through the lens of humanity; they frame situations in the context of how people—not processes or things—are affected. T1s from more of a self-centered perspective, where they are drawn to others to fill their own innate need for rubbing shoulders or networking for a new job or sales prospect, and T2s from a more outward-directed, altruistic perspective.

And here's the most important part of all, the good news for all of us. It's a choice. People People are made, not born. Okay . . . some, it seems, are born with it. In recent years scientists have discovered a strong neurological relationship among social people, those we might consider Type I People People; they have more gray matter in specific parts of their brains than nonsocial people. This could suggest that you're either born a People Person or not, which may explain why some people do seem to come by Type I traits naturally, like public speaking or picking up girls at the mall. But it doesn't mean those traits can't be learned and refined by practice. Some are born with a natural gift for music or art, but even those that aren't can still learn those disciplines and become quite proficient.

The attributes of People People are often referred to as "soft skills" or "people skills," the very word *skills* connoting a learned behavior or ability. Learning professionals and company training departments have long made soft skills and leadership training available to their workforce. Why do organizations even care? Because they understand the natural connection between happy, balanced people at home and productive, engaged (read "profitable") employees at work.

Recently, while attempting to book some flights for a family vacation, a Delta Air Lines agent, Fritata (not her real name, or anyone's for that matter), patiently worked with me to find the very best deals. She used her vast knowledge of "the system" to explore various possibilities and flight combinations that aren't normally accessible to the everyday, online customer. This took more time than would normally be acceptable in the quick turnaround environment of a busy call center. But she knew she could manipulate a few variables to get a better price, using a backdoor approach that even not all agents knew about. Soon Fritata cheerily announced that she had arranged a very cost-friendly deal for me and my family of seven.

Why would she do that? We'd never met before and I hadn't bribed her or played a sympathy or celebrity author card (only actual celebrity authors regularly get away with that anyway, like J. K. Rowling or William Shakespeare). What could she have possibly gained by pulling a few strings for a total stranger, a non–celebrity author like me?

Maybe she was just in a good mood that day. Just feeling nice. Or perhaps my Plutonium Level Frequent Flyer status popped up on her screen and her clever display of string-pulling was just one of the rewards of elite membership. It's also possible that she works on an incentive or commission plan and her working the system was nothing more than a little show to dupe me into believing I was getting the special (wink, wink) *Plutonium* deal. I am, after all, an easy target—a bit of a simpleton, really.

But isn't it possible that Fritata, unlike myriad monotone peers plugged into telephone headsets who mostly seem put off by the very idea that I would call them to seek assistance, actually *enjoys* working with and taking care of people?

More to the point, could it be that this agent was a shining example of Delta's rigorous agent training program that places a heavy emphasis on customer satisfaction and on being well spoken, with a polite, engaging and patient personality—i.e., People People qualities that she *learned* through training, regardless of any natural predisposition she may have already had?

A savvy, trained Delta agent with Type I people skills *and* a Type II passion for complete customer care will sometimes take a few liberties with the system to close a deal, and by so doing sows seeds of continued customer loyalty. A People Person will strive to honor and obey policies, regulations and standards, but keeps an open mind and understands the spirit of the law.

The Spirit of the Law

The following story isn't necessarily entirely untrue, nor does it not completely include names, places and situations that may or may not have not happened.

It is winter 1981. A nine-year-old boy named Marcus goes to a police bicycle auction in suburban Philadelphia with one dollar and the dream of owning his very first bike. His parents could never afford to buy him a new one, and with the money he has saved from chores he determines that he'd be thrilled even with a used one.

He eyes the inventory and sees a handful of surprisingly clean and shiny bikes that he likes. The auction begins with the most beautiful blue bike the boy has ever seen. But the opening bids are too high. He doesn't have enough to even try for it. Bid after bid, bikes are sold for well below market prices, but far beyond the boy's ability to pay. As the number and quality of bicycles dwindle, the auctioneer notices Marcus's face getting longer and sadder as the boy holds his single dollar bill in both hands as if praying for a miracle.

After an hour of bikes being sold before his eyes, only one tiny, dented, cruddy bike remains. It's the boy's last shot at leaving with a bicycle. The auctioneer calls out, "Who will give me *one dollar* for this final bicycle?"

Marcus looks up, a glimmer of hope and a tear in his eyes. In a shaky voice he raises his dollar bill, "I will. I have a dollar!"

A kind smile spreads across the auctioneer's face. He looks down at Marcus and says, "I've got a one dollar bid from the young man up front here!" Marcus's heart skips a beat as he realizes what's happening.

A brief moment of silent anticipation passes as the boy's eyes meet the auctioneer's. Marcus can hardly believe it. He looks at his hard-earned dollar bill, gives it a little kiss and beams at the auctioneer . . . who has since turned away and without skipping a beat barks out, "*Five* dollars! Can I hear *five* dollars for this last bike of the day?"

Tough break, kid.

You see, civic government regulations and police department policy are clear that "no confiscated item will be sold for less than half its assessed value," and a *dollar* for even an old, beat-up Schwinn? Not enough to pay for the banana seat, pal.

If you were sure that this story was heading toward a happy, miracle ending in which the auctioneer sells the boy the bike for one dollar, then you may indeed have some People People leanings bubbling inside you. Because that's exactly what you'd expect someone in an authoritative position to do: put *people,* not rules *first.* But as a rule, People People aren't scofflaws and policy breakers. They must use proper judgment and weigh decisions like these carefully. They are responsible, conscientious citizens and coworkers. Their people-first focus isn't just for individuals but includes entire communities, workgroups or associations of people. The auctioneer may very well be the sweetest man you'll ever meet, but he was just doing his job, right?

True as that may be, if you agree with it and find the outcome of the story appropriate, you may need to engage the services of a baying pack of bloodhounds to hunt down and tree your missing heart, because the auctioneer clearly misunderstands the "spirit of the law" concept.

Here then is the actual ending to the story, at least as we've heard it told or not told . . .

CHAPTER THREE

A brief moment of silent anticipation passes as the boy's eyes meet the auctioneer's. Marcus can hardly believe it. He looks at his hard-earned dollar bill, gives it a little kiss and beams at the auctioneer . . . who has since turned away and without skipping a beat barks out, "*Five* dollars—can I hear *five* dollars for this last bike of the day?"

Marcus lowers his head, stuffs his precious dollar in the bib pocket of his overalls and fights tears. The auction continues.

"Five dollars, I've got five dollars, can I see seven? Seven dollars, thank you sir. Eight. Eight. Who will give me eight for this wonderful Schwinn bicycle—last one of the lot?" Each bid is like a dagger in Marcus's soul.

"Okay, I'm looking for ten dollars, ten dollars . . . going once, twice, *sold!*" the auctioneer bellows quickly without waiting for another bid. Marcus doesn't bother looking to see who won the beautiful blue bike. "*Sold!* To the young man down front for ten dollars!"

The auctioneer steps off the little stage and heads right to Marcus. He squats down to the boy's eye level, reaches around back to his pocket and pulls out his wallet. He carefully counts out nine dollars and extends them toward a now stunned Marcus.

"I noticed you never bid more than a dollar all day, so I figure that must be all you have. Here you go. Now you have ten," the auctioneer says. "The bike is yours."

On a mid-January Saturday afternoon in Philadelphia, nine-year-old Marcus, all 4 feet 5 inches and sixty-eight pounds of skin and bones, wraps his little arms around the auctioneer's midsection and cries like a baby in front of a few dozen auction bidders. "Thank you, thank you, thank you," Marcus sobs.

People People values are learnable attributes that can be internalized until they become second nature. It is the great challenge of human existence—to learn and develop, to progress, to improve. To better ourselves and our station. The simple truth is by learning to focus outward, on others, we improve ourselves. As in the example above, sometimes this outward focus requires taking liberties with convention, at a possible risk or cost to oneself.

Where are you on the People People continuum?

Maybe you are the nicest person in town: a philanthropist, a volunteer and helper to the helpless. But no one can understand a word you're saying. You're too quiet, shy and introverted. You have few friends and don't really have much fun. You freeze up when asked to address a group and your credibility falters. You would do well to come out of your shell and improve your public persona.

Or perhaps you face a different challenge. For all of your gregariousness, cheer and joviality, you still seem to have hit a wall. Your skills are valued in certain settings and you've reaped a few rewards and advantages for them at work, home and elsewhere. But there is a limit to your growth, development and success. Becoming a real People Person holds vastly more promise and potential, as you develop and demonstrate real concern for others.

And for thousands of organizations, small, large and gigantic, with employees spread across the globe in every time zone and culture, there are parallel challenges and rewards. A company can spend gobs of money to provide the pay, perks and prizes (an organizational Type I effort) that would qualify them, on paper, as an amazing and caring employer. But without ascending to the next level of genuinely putting their people first (Type II effort), they limit their own organizational growth, development and success.

CHAPTER FOUR
Companies That CARE

People People are the backbone of the best organizations, the spine of successful businesses, the vertebral column of winning companies.

The Great Place to Work Institute, known for its annual rankings of the "Best Companies to Work for in America" published in *Fortune* magazine, has identified key characteristics of managers in "best" or "great" work cultures—*trust, respect, credibility* and *fairness*—and each characteristic describes *how* managers are as *people* and not *what* they do as *managers*.

Trust is the real aim according to the Great Place folks, with respect, credibility and fairness identified as leadership qualities that help build trust. They've concluded that trust is at the very heart of what makes a place like Google, DreamWorks or Mercedes-Benz USA three of America's best places to work. It's not just the cachet of the brand that makes them great places to work or increases employee loyalty; it's the care the company demonstrates for their people.[1]

Given what you've learned thus far about People People, specifically T2s and T3s, do you think *they* would be more likely to build trust in a workplace than Everyone Else, including Jerks? It seems reasonable that non-self-absorbed, service-focused associates and leaders would do more to build a trusting environment for coworkers than aggressive, autocratic bosses, regardless of how impressive their brand, market share or expertise may be.

High-Tech People

For a decade, Google's prevailing managerial philosophy was to leave people alone; let the engineers do their jobs and if they ever needed any help they could ask their bosses, whose technical expertise was ostensibly good enough to get them a manager's job in the first place. In 2009, Google launched its own in-house investigations called Project Oxygen to determine a short list of characteristics for being a great manager at Google.

After analyzing a mountain of performance reviews, feedback surveys and nominations for top manager awards the "people analytics" team came back with eight rules for effective Google managers that wouldn't shock anyone within a thousand miles of the Great Place to Work Institute: be a good coach, express interest in your team's success and well-being, be a good communicator, and other "soft" factors that *build trust* scored the highest. Ranking dead last, the eighth (of eight) most important factor, was the manager's technical expertise. At *Google*? What employees valued most were even-keeled bosses who made time for one-on-one meetings, who helped people puzzle through problems by asking questions, not dictating answers, and who took an interest in employees' lives and careers.

In short, managers who are People People.

Even Google's VP of people operations (HR), Laszlo Bock, was surprised. "In the Google context, we'd always believed that to be a manager, particularly on the engineering side, you need to be as deep or deeper a technical expert than the people who work for you," Bock said. "It turns out that that's absolutely the least important thing. It's important, but pales in comparison. Much more important is just making that connection and being accessible."[2]

For this "Best Company" (No. 1 in 2012), it's not the pay or the perks or the prestige, but literally how well people are treated by other people, in this case their manager. Do pay and perks and prestige play a role? Of course. In fact, hard benefits are the tangible expressions of how much or little an organization cares for its people. But by themselves, pay, perks and prestige simply aren't enough. People People understand this and go beyond the green.

Great Place's contention is that without trust the piles of perks mean little. It's that human touch that is too often overlooked, even by well-meaning, often very generous employers. There must be trust.

And respect. We'll flesh out respect a bit later, but for now it's significant to point out that respect, like fairness, is an internally developed and generated characteristic. A Type II People Person quality, if you will. For company leaders at any level, it's *who* and *how* you are, not how much you pay or if you install pool tables in every break room, that ultimately qualifies your company as a great place to work or even marks you as a great boss.

People First

Ultimate Software (company motto: "People First"), headquartered in Weston, Florida, was No. 25 on the 2012 list of best large companies to work for. What put them there? More employees, for one. Until they eclipsed the 1,000 head count mark they had to settle for merely being the No. 1 best *medium* company in America to work for . . . two years in a row. Before that they were ranked No. 3, twice. Now, with almost 1,500 employees they rub shoulders with the big boys of the best places to work, like Intel (44,000), Marriott (108,000) and Starbucks (109,000). Okay, so maybe they rub ankles. Still, they're in the same category.

Minimum head count aside, what makes Ultimate Software *great*? Because when it comes to being a great company, the kind where people feel connected and engaged, size isn't everything. According to Scott Scherr, founder and CEO, it's a combination of tangibles and intangibles.

For starters, Ultimate provides 100 percent insurance coverage for employees and their families. "I believe there are very few companies out there who provide that," Scherr told me. He's right. In fact there are only a handful that do it even among the 2012 list of best companies. Ultimate Software also contributes an unheard of 30 percent match on employee 401(k)s, with *no cap*. Every employee has company equity. Now those are some tangibles.

More evidence of Ultimate's commitment to people is taken straight from their Web site:

> *As individuals and as corporate citizens, the people of Ultimate Software also work to make a difference in our community. We firmly believe in doing the right thing and making a difference, starting locally. That's evidenced by our contributions of time and money to charitable organizations . . ."*[3]

And it goes on to list sixteen organizations they contribute to.

"We give a percentage of our total revenue to charities, even in hard times," Scherr said. "And the company matches all charitable donations made by employees."

Vivian Maza, Ultimate's chief people officer, added, "And that just scratches the surface. There's way more that we do for others and our own people that doesn't get attention."

As an organization, Ultimate really strives to live their people-first philosophy. And they've done it since day one. When Scherr quit his job with a large payroll company to start his own shop in 1990, he set the bar high. "I brought in three people that I knew and gave them equity right from the start," he said. "I had the company pay 100 percent benefits right from the start. We still do that for all of our people now and we're up over 1,500 [employees]. I don't see it much different from those three people. Now, instead of three we have 1,500 families to take care of."

Maza was one of the three people Scherr asked to join him in his adventure. "It was an easy decision," she said to me. "Even though we didn't even have a product at the time; we didn't know what we had. But a lot of people trusted Scott so much that they'd be willing to do anything for him. He's just such a humble, hard-working, caring man that people want to work with him."

Is Scherr's commitment to people really the same as it was when they started? Is that even possible, given their growth in just two decades?

"From the very beginning and until today, we just believe in doing the right thing," Maza said. "You can have all the benefits and the ice cream truck and $250 per child per year for sports sponsorships and jerseys, but those aren't 'business decisions.' They're 'people decisions.' People can tell that we're sincere."

They must be. In order to take care of 1,500 employees and their families means that they can't afford to pay outrageous salaries, yet Ultimate employees have taken pay cuts just to come aboard. They recognize a truly good deal when they see it.

The company's commitment to its people principles is unwavering, and the business is better for it. "We've never had a single layoff," Scherr said. "We went public in 1998 and our stock was at $10. In 1999 it was $15. In 2000 it dropped to $2. But we didn't change any benefits at all. Our people didn't quit on us at the time. We got through it. In 2008, it was at $40 and it's at about $90 today."

From a market growth perspective, the company is worth $2.5 billion. For Scherr and his leadership team, doing the right thing paid off. But the financial return was never the motivation, just the reward.

"Why do it? I think it was how I was brought up. It's who I am," Scherr admitted. But he was also happy to concede, "And it's just good business, frankly. . . . When people are attracted to an environment where they know you're taking care of them and their family, they'll do anything to take care of you. I think it translates into products and services, which is what happened with Ultimate. I've said all along 'let's just stick together and we'll make our products better, our services better and it will build a company that can take of our families.'

"We started with four of us sharing two cubicles. And it grew to 5, 7, 10, 20, 100, up to 1,500, but the culture has stayed the same since the very beginning and it hasn't changed."

How does Ultimate Software manage to keep the culture vibrant and consistent with Scherr's vision in the face of an ever-increasing and more diverse workforce? Simply put, they jealously guard the culture and make sure they are hiring competent professionals that share the same people-first mentality.

"You can't get in [be hired by Ultimate] if you don't have the skills, but one of our 'competencies' is a personality," Scherr said. "They need to fit in with who we are as people and what we do as a company. I'll ask myself, 'Would you want to have this person over for Thanksgiving?' I wouldn't hire the most successful person in the world if he didn't have character. It would be like a cancer. Like Terrell Owens [American football star]. He's great individually, but he can't be part of a team.

"Call it good karma," Scherr said. "The more we take care of our people and their families, the more good people seek us out and want to be part of our family." This allows Ultimate to be pickier in their hiring. "I recently had a telephone conversation with a very senior-level person on the West Coast, who's dying to come work with us," Scherr said. "He thinks we're the next big thing. He wants to make a difference, too. He wants to leave his company of 100,000 employees and move back East with us."

Using a people-first blueprint, as personally modeled by Scherr, Maza and the rest of their handpicked leadership team, recruiters and hiring managers are careful to hire those who fit the description, helping to ensure the survival of the culture. Even still, Scherr and his senior team still find the time and opportunities to apply their personal touch as frequently as they can to preserve the spirit of people first.

Pamela Iverson, a fifteen-year employee in the HR Department, said, "Senior executives really care about me and my family. There are so many instances that are less evident [than fully paid health coverage] and profoundly more personal. For example, two summers ago, our mid-year [off-site meeting] was in Aspen, Colorado. Shortly after arriving, my husband began to get short of breath from the altitude. We had a cocktail reception that afternoon, and I was mentioning this to someone as Scott Scherr joined our conversation. He told us that he found it very helpful to have a bottle of oxygen in the room to make it easier to sleep. We thought nothing more of it, and went on to enjoy our evening. When my husband and I returned to our room that night, a bottle of oxygen had been delivered, with a note from Scott, wishing my husband a good night's sleep."

It's those little touches, particularly ones made by the CEO and his ilk, that really reinforce "People First."

Camden Property Trust, with almost 1,700 employees, was 2012's sixth Best Company to Work For. It's no surprise that "Camden's people make the difference," Jennifer Altizer, a seven-year employee, said. "Recently, a coworker called me from the parking garage to let me know I had a flat tire. Even though it was after normal business hours and he was headed to the Camden Happy Hour, he offered to help put on the spare. That evening I had not one, but four Camden employees offer to help!! Two coworkers went out of their way to help put the spare tire on my car (after 5 p.m. and when both had other obligations), and two others offered to help in any way possible. As a single mom, it's nice to know that I have coworkers who will look out for me. Camden takes care of its employees with its benefits, perks, and amazing company culture, and Camden employees take care of each other."

Margaret Plummer, Camden's VP of employee relations, told me, "Camden cares for its people, but our caring culture is possible only because our people also care for each other," she said. "Policies and programs do not create exceptional work environments; people do. Our associates choose every day to make Camden a great place to work."

Bottom line?

Great companies are awash in People People; they are the medulla oblongata of the best places to work, the spinal fluid of wildly successful organizations, the—you get the idea. And more than just adding a little sunshine to their coworkers' day, People People's efforts can have a measurable impact on personal and professional goals, strategies and business outcomes.

Rocky Mountain High

Take Brian Callahan, the director of fun at New Belgium Brewing. This rapidly growing craft brewery in Fort Collins, Colorado, has wholeheartedly embraced a people culture of transparency and collaboration. In 1991, Callahan, an aspiring brewmeister, was the first employee of the company. Cofounders Jeff Lebesch and Kim Jordan offered Callahan ownership in the business because "it seemed like the right thing to do." As Callahan's role with the fledgling company has evolved from brewing to operations to his current position, he has witnessed the development of the brewery's reputation of doing the right thing—for the environment (New Belgium operates off of wind power), for their loyal fan base of customers and of course for their own people.

"There are many things we do because it's the right thing to do. For example, we just know that having fun is an essential ingredient to our culture, it's one of our core values and beliefs. Of course it's not all fun and games; we have to be profitable in order to stay in business," Callahan said. "A lot of studies show that happy workers are more productive workers and we can translate productivity to our bottom line."

Here's what that means to the company: New Belgium's production volume in 1991 was 225 thirty-one-gallon barrels, or the rough equivalent of enough beer for one standard dorm party at the University of Colorado Boulder. Twenty years later, annual volume is closing in on a million barrels, they employ over 400 engaged beer lovers and annual revenue is $140 million.[4] Remember, this was just a couple of friends who wanted to make a difference, have fun and do right by the environment.

"This culture is one of openness and sharing so people help each other. Because our culture engenders an ownership mentality and an entrepreneurial spirit we are able to keep up an assertive growth rate that provides lots of opportunity," Callahan added. But how does the brewery maintain a people-friendly culture as it continues expanding? "Our recognition as a best place to work from *Outside* magazine, the *Wall Street Journal,* and the WorldBlu survey allows us to draw from large pools of candidates so that we can hire the best available people."

Sounds a lot like Ultimate Software's story, doesn't it? A growing company with a people focus that actually puts *people* first—sharing, collaborating, socializing—not *just* the creation of people programs, fun initiatives, reward trips and other tangibles. It's the day-to-day human interactions that define the culture. That's what People People contribute to any company.

New Belgium boasts a 97 percent employee retention rate. People come to Fort Collins to stay. For many, it's a dream gig. A worker on the brewery floor told me that he gets up each day and comes to a job where he makes "the best beer in the world, with the best people I know. These guys are amazing to work for. And the area is ideal." Though some have pulled up their roots and headed east, the quaint craft brewery's growth fueled a demand for a more national footprint. Another brewery is under construction in Ashville, North Carolina, and will be operational in 2015.

In order to build and maintain clearly defined people cultures, small and mid-sized organizations like New Belgium Brewing, Ultimate Software and Camden Property Trust rely on strong Type II or even Type III (where they exist) senior leaders to model the behaviors, and a rigorous filtering process to find candidates that fit in.

"For any one position, there might be multiple candidates with the skills to do the job," Camden's Plummer told me. "Our approach to finding the candidate with the right culture fit is about creating multiple touch points: A career site focused on our culture; a pre-employment assessment that measures culture fit; multiple interview levels; reference checks; and post-interview discussions about candidate choice all create multiple opportunities to determine whether a candidate will fit with Camden's culture. Of course, the process does not end with the hire. New associates continue to learn about our culture through their teams, mentors, leadership and cultural events to help them be successful at Camden and continue to build our culture."

CHAPTER FIVE
More Companies That CARE

In February 2012, Microsoft ran an ad campaign that pitched its products as treating people (customers) better than Google's did. At that time Google had adopted some privacy policies about their e-mail and other online services that had many users concerned and reconsidering their brand loyalty. Microsoft released some print ads that featured in large, highlighted text, "Putting people first." Beneath the headline, the ad explained how Google had deprioritized their users' desires for protecting their e-mails and Web searches in favor of pleasing Google's advertising customers. The ad also described Microsoft's suite of online tools, stressing protection and privacy, and invited those who felt that Google's changes had "rubbed them the wrong way" to consider coming over (or back) to Microsoft. The heart of the message was that Microsoft's products provide a level of privacy that shows the company's concern for people, making the users' protection a priority over other business interests. In other words, Microsoft's claim was that they put people first, and Google did not.[1]

People *Second*?

In this case the people are customers. And as market shares among tech companies are reduced by upstart competitors, customer care is paramount as a differentiator. It's all about the customer experience, isn't it? But what about Google's *own* people, their employees? Are *they* second to business interests as well? And what about Microsoft? How do they prioritize *their* people? As critical as customer service is, it simply won't happen externally until it's happening internally first. It's a "pay it forward" concept, isn't it? Customer service skills can be taught and learned, but even the desire to apply those skills in a real-world setting with live customers really depends less on ability than attitude.

On paper, there's little room to dispute that both Microsoft and Google, from an organizational perspective, care about their own people. Both tech giants have long been considered "Best Companies to Work For," spending millions of dollars on benefits packages, retirement funds matching, bonus programs, incentives, world-class cafeterias, day-care centers, wellness programs and health clubs, game rooms, parties, lunches, awards and recognition and on and on. Both companies are also on the list of "World's Most Admired Companies" because of their relentless innovation, social and environmental awareness and bottom-line results.

But we've already learned what Google employees really want, from their managers at least—more Type II traits. They want People People for bosses. It isn't much of a reach to guess that it's the same story at Microsoft, and indeed every other large organization, in any industry.

Perks and benefits may not necessarily be a true indication of the heart of a company. Many large organizations launch full speed into building what they believe to be people-focused cultures by excitedly bricklaying all the tangible benefits without establishing a strong foundation of internalized People People principles among their management. They put the style before the substance, the T1 without the T2. For them it is nothing more than a business strategy.

Consider, for example, how flat employee recognition falls in the absence of sincerity, a values-based purpose and a relationship of trust. A company can dole out the freebies, but it's no guarantee that employees actually *feel* appreciated or recognized (more on recognition later). People People don't rely on the toy to express the attaboy (I meant that to rhyme), especially in recent economic times when most budgets are too tight for trinkets, spiffs and giveaways anyway.

It's important to remember a few things about "Best Companies" and "Great Companies" and all the lists and publications. The companies that are included and ranked on annual lists of fabulous workplaces are paying clients of, for example, the Great Place to Work Institute. They have, in effect, nominated themselves, and by so doing subject their organizations to a pretty rigorous battery of surveys and audits to determine their level of greatness. None of these measures are free. They pay the fees to apply. Those companies that qualify as "great" and make the "best" lists enjoy the attendant attention and the cachet of being a great company to work for, and not just a good one. It raises their profile and public image. It becomes a recruiting tool. It gives a competitive advantage as their market visibility and awareness increase.

But the truth is, not all great companies are officially recognized as "Great Companies." Thousands and thousands of organizations worldwide fall outside the net, many of which enjoy all the rewards of living with a people-first focus. Costco, BMW, Southwest Airlines, Sony, Nike and other big brands aren't on the list, but all enjoy reputations of strong cultures. And let's be honest: not all "Great Companies" really *are* great companies to work for, regardless of audit results.

Why not? The company perks themselves are easy to measure and evaluate. And great care is taken to assess employee opinions objectively. Still, one wonders: the company, with its many flavors of beneficence, may be people focused, but are the *people* people focused? It is one thing for the company to show its appreciation and respect for you. But what about the company's *people*? What about its leaders? Its managers? When

Portnoy Porcelain and Piping proclaims that its core values are respect, integrity, safety, excellence and fun, do they mean that their people actually espouse, embody and endeavor to *live* those values as *individuals,* or just that collectively they all really think those are great values that someday it would be cool if somebody, somewhere lived?

Accountable People

Therein lies the warm massage-oil rub. People People are the ones that take upon themselves the personal accountability to actually *live* the company values, not just claim to espouse them. The coziness and familial feel of smaller, newer companies make it somewhat easier to recruit, hire and nurture the kind of worker that reinforces the people culture. Accessibility and proximity make monitoring and repairing the culture easier as well.

But for larger companies, it is supercritical that employees at every level and position take this to heart: it is individuals, not the stated mission of the company or even the collective conscience of the workforce, who are responsible for building a positive and productive culture. It's the people themselves who must demonstrate respect and integrity or safety and excellence in order for the company to claim an adherence to such values. Millions of employees, all over the world, lack the needed personal commitment to truly contribute to an organization's culture, to *give* to the company and its mission rather than take. Legion are the "expectors" who proudly proclaim what a fantastic employer they have, such an amazing array of benefits and perks, great pay and strong values, and yet they themselves are mean-spirited, conniving, deceptive and insincere. The lengths to which a *company* goes in an effort to feather the nest and provide the right atmosphere in which their employees can thrive are often inversely matched by the great lengths that many spoiled, demanding *employees* go to ruin it all.

Though the burden does rest on everyone's shoulders, it's true that managers wield the most influence in building a strong, authentic people culture. It's not uncommon for the leadership of an organization to use the company's better-than-generous pay and benefits plan as an excuse to carry on like ogres with their employees. It's as if they think, "You can afford to have me berate and belittle you, to ignore your passion and great ideas, to demean your efforts in front of your peers and treat you like an idiot because, dammit, this is a *great company to work for!* I mean *look at your paycheck!*" Even if the manager who thought that were endowed from head to toe in Type I people skills, it would still be a painful stretch and an affront to the institution to extend the title of People Person to him or her.

Reaping and Sowing

Many organizations strongly tout their focus on customer care. Too often they, or more significantly their managers, skip the most important step of putting their own people first, and customers usually are the eventual victim. Treat the cable installer well at work and he's more likely to treat a customer well when installing their cable channels. (There's no proof that he'll give the customer premium channels for free, but maybe an extra ESPN channel or two). Show some respect to hourly fast-food workers and watch how less frequently they contribute personal biological outputs to the special sauce. A little laughter and the occasional bit of praise or recognition in a call center will do wonders to the tone and tenor of the customer service calls those college freshmen are making for you.

Still, a shockingly large number of managers can't seem to comprehend the "law of the harvest" by putting their own people first and showing them the same respect they hope will be shown to clients.

A very large retailer with an incredible reputation for customer service is a good example. Here are just a few anonymous comments, posted for all the world to see on Glassdoor, from hundreds of dissatisfied current and former employees throughout the United States:

"Nice place to shop, not so nice to work." . . . *California*

"Excellent customer service, yet horrible service of employees."
    . . . Tennessee

"Managers don't care about your personal life." . . . *Maryland*

*"Managers will talk down to you in a condescending manner. Managers
    make it hard to communicate with them by being 'unavailable.'"*
    . . . Florida

*"They treat the customers well, the same cannot be said for the employees.
    I refuse to shop there now, and before I was a die-hard customer."*
    . . . California

"The [founders/owners] have no idea what happens in their stores."
    . . . Arizona

*"I was told that they are people first, however at [my store], they are not.
    Each manager was there looking out for themselves only, even if it
    hurt the department and the store; which is no way to run a good
    business."* . . . *Illinois*

*"Reevaluate the [store] culture. Management doesn't hold the same ideals
    it used to."* . . . *California*

*"[The company] pretends to be a great place to work when in reality the
    management does not connect well with the employees."* . . . *Las Vegas*

That's some pretty surprising feedback for a large national chain that
has spent a lot of time on both the "Best Companies" and the "Most
Admired" lists. It started as a small family business, and the family is still
actively involved. It built a reputation for outstanding customer service,
empowering employees to use their best judgment in serving the customer. It enjoys amazing stories of customer care . . . but no real sense of
employee care. Is it just a case of a few squeaky wheels? First, there are
hundreds more with similar comments. And second, even among those
employees who call themselves "very satisfied" we find these remarks:

*"Going above and beyond for your customer tends to go unnoticed most
of the time. . . . When you really take care of your customer and
problem-solve to get the customer what they need and more, it almost
never gets recognized, which is demoralizing in a sense. It smacks at
the very pride the company developed in you about customer loyalty."
. . . California*

"Too much favoritism." . . . Texas

*"The commission structure is such that it makes it nearly impossible to
form a team concept. There is no ethical protocol between associates!
They will take your returning clients if you allow it!" . . . California*

*"Management was horrible, but HR and store managers did not seem to
care." . . . Washington*

Individual Commitment in the Big Leagues

Inevitably, the sheer size of a company will dilute its original culture. As ranks swell, diversity increases, and backgrounds, philosophies and personal values multiply. The notion that a strong culture can survive massive workforce growth, at least in its pure, original state, is ludicrous.

Communicating the culture to the workforce is, however difficult, totally possible. Using the full complement of modern communications tools and technologies, committed and hardworking internal communications and people departments can reasonably expect a high degree of reach. Regular touches with the workforce by trained management can account for much of the communication of values, culture and expectations. It is a monumental challenge and an exciting task.

High employee retention rates are critical to a push for cultural consistency, and the revolving door of turnover, compounded by the diluted state of the culture, stymies much of the progress as leaders find themselves forever starting over with the process. Most organizations understand the need to recruit and hire according to their stated values, whether they be people focused or not, but larger companies with hundreds or even thousands of positions that must be filled urgently don't have the luxury of a stringent "people filter" and must settle for hiring talent with skills only (and often not even those), leaving the training on values and culture for some other time, thus perpetuating the cycle.

Companies that lavish their employees with all manner of benefits and bonuses, free lunches and massages, but do little to actually cultivate people first, also run the risk of spoiling their staff. A spirit of entitlement overpowers a spirit of gratitude and the pure material benefits of working for the organization become the motivation. In difficult economic circumstances, when these tangibles are in danger of disappearing or are the first to be dropped, employee morale, loyalty and output decline as pessimism and dissatisfaction rise.

The need for individual accountability, for people like you and me to commit to practicing people-first principles, has never been greater. Okay, it's probably been greater, especially when you consider entire periods in human history of abject evil, darkness and ignorance. The '60s come to mind. But the need is at least as great now as it's ever been.

True people-first organizations build a spirit among the ranks that is less likely to be ruffled in the face of challenges. This people spirit is in fact a reward unto itself. The esprit de corps, the fun, the trust, the respect, the honesty and authenticity among the personnel provide more lasting joy than the temporary excitement of the paycheck or the holiday turkey. Put the two together and you've really got something.

For the millions who have worked alongside miserable and complaining associates, the idea of working in a People People atmosphere makes getting up each day easier. Going to work at a job where they have a friend, where they enjoy autonomy and freedom to do their best work, where their skills and goals are matched well with their duties and, above all, where people respect each other regardless of title, position, pay or background is a greater reward than the higher pay they might have had at their last job, where they toiled alongside total Jerks.

A longtime acquaintance of mine, who had mentored me in some ways, once came to me for a job. I told him I didn't have anything available that was equal to his experience. He had held several senior-level positions in his career. He said he'd be happy to make less money to "just be a teammate," to report to me and to not have any direct reports, and to be part of a culture that was a reward of its own.

Too many unhappy people stay put in jobs because of money and personal or family financial security. Another close friend of mine called me up and said, "I'm done. I can't do it anymore." He had been with a large company for five years and had even recently been promoted. The company was well known for its commitment to client care, community service and, most importantly, its loyalty to employees. Paying above-market wages and generous benefits, the company leaders espoused family values and building a culture of praise and recognition.

But politics, infighting, power struggles and personal clashes were all too frequent. They had a taken a major toll on morale and my friend had had enough. He was miserable . . . but well paid. I asked him if he had already quit and had found another job. His response? "Oh, gosh no, but I'm looking," he admitted. "But believe me, the second I find something that can meet our needs, *I am outta here!* Until then . . . I just can't *afford* to leave."

How sad it is that while he unhappily hangs on to his well-paying job, neither he nor his employer are truly benefitting. He can't stand what he's doing and the company is paying good money for him to do it (or not).

Diamonds in the Rough

Of course it's not all pessimism and darkness in large corporate settings. People People are found in companies of all sizes and always strive to spread a positive influence. Statistically speaking, you have to expect even more People Peeps in a larger workforce. The truly great companies find these jewels and recognize their contributions to the culture. They pick them out and hold them up for others to model. "This is what we want the rest of you to be like," they say.

One of Marriott International's core values is "Put People First." And they mean their *own* people: "Around the globe, we offer our *associates* fair treatment, respect, and opportunities for personal and professional growth."[2] Sure, they have a strong customer focus; but it starts with their people. The company highlights outstanding individual contributions of employees that truly live the people-first value. Here's how they described just one of these People People:

> *Working at the front desk of the Courtyard Nashville Downtown, Rick Collins likens his job to a bartender, but without the drinks. He's always ready and willing to listen to a guest's story. He's never too busy to take a moment and connect with a guest, whether it's by giving the tie off his neck to a businessman who forgot his or calling ahead to restaurants to help ensure his international guests get a Nashville welcome.*
>
> *Taking care of guests is only one part of Rick's job. He makes it his personal mission to put a smile on the face of every associate in the hotel, too. From the minute he arrives at work, Rick is greeting and fist-bumping associates all the way from housekeeping to the front desk. His easy way with associates has earned him the role of primary trainer for the front desk. He calls his trainees "Rickadee's Chickadees," taking new associates under his wing, helping them adapt to the fast pace of the front desk and the ever-changing needs of guests. As a result, the hotel's guest service scores ranked #5 out of 58 managed Courtyard hotels in the Southern region for 2011.*
>
> *For much of the last 14 years, Rick has faced serious health issues. But that hasn't stopped him looking for ways to serve others. He's the coach of two "Able Bodies" softball teams, providing an environment where disabled kids can thrive. The mother of one of the boys on his team recently told Rick the experience has helped her son's self-esteem so much that he has his first*

friend at school. Wanting to encourage and support this young player, Rick bought the boy a cape and dubbed him the team's superhero.

After a recent bout of illness that had Rick in the hospital over Christmas, he had so many visitors from his hotel and the community he thought he'd never get any rest! Their love and positive support helped him recover and get him back to the job he loves. Asked why he loves his job so much, Rick matter-of-factly responds, "These are my people. This is my family here. Why wouldn't I love to help my family?"[3]

The burden of a truly caring culture rests squarely on individual shoulders. Employees own the culture, especially among large multinationals and internationally franchised companies. The scaling of corporate culture is a massive undertaking from a centralized office. The culture must first be envisioned and enabled by leadership, then individuals take responsibility to see that it sinks in and remains anchored. When Bill Marriott Sr. opened his first few hotels it was easy to agree upon and live certain values. Marriott's commitment to employee care, a people-first mentality, was still in its purest form and easier to execute. But through rapid growth it became incumbent upon those who followed to replicate those values, truly live them, as the footprint of the company expanded. Today, over 100,000 individual Marriott employees must take it upon themselves to follow Bill Jr.'s counsel to connect with each other as people.

"Greet your people. Talk to them. Ask about their families," Marriott said. "Get to know them on as personal a level as they'll allow. It'll make all the difference."

CHAPTER SIX
People People and Authenticity

Growing up, I dreamed of being an actor, a comedian, a news reporter, a sports anchor or anything that would allow me to entertain other people. When I determined in my teen years that I had a face made for radio, I figured that course would probably be my best bet. (My mother, of course, vehemently disagreed. Ah, moms.) Plus, I loved news and information. My sister Andrea taught me to read when I was three years old and I dove right in. Not content with Dick and Jane and Curious George, I was able to read at about a ninth-grade level in kindergarten, and so I read whatever textbook or novel was within reach. My uncanny abilities also gave me a taste of public attention at a very young age.

"Go ahead, give him something to read," my proud mother would say to aunts, uncles, sometimes total strangers. "He can read anything. He's a genius." Someone would inevitably reach for the nearest newspaper and soon I would be reading stock reports and international politics to the amusement of all. "The kid's barely out of diapers!" someone might comment. (All geniuses have their flaws.)

I was tickled by their fawning, but I gained something else. I had a knack for reading aloud, for interpreting copy well, capturing the author's original intent. I made it sound natural and conversational. I didn't stutter, flub words, slur or sound monotone or robotic. I could see ahead and read the entire paragraph in my mind before I ever intoned the words. Knowing where the story was going made it easy to find the most natural tempo, tone and tenor. I soon discovered this level of expertise was not very common among other children my age, and to this day it is still a gift that has served me well.

Unfortunately, I also discovered that, as far as having a career in radio went, a gift I did not possess was "the voice." I grew up in an age when radio was still a vibrant, profitable medium. Announcers and DJs in those days had deep, rich, full manly voices that vibrated the speakers and emasculated every male within a mile of the stereo. A lot of "jocks" were the scrawniest, nerdiest-looking doofuses I'd ever seen, but boy did they have some *pipes*. They adopted standard American accents that left no hint of their region of origin. Radio ads were slick and professional. As a teen I felt discouraged because I've always had kind of a soft, scratchy, airy, testosterone-deprived-sounding voice. Not Michael Jackson, mind you, but Michael J. Fox wouldn't be a reach.

But change, like death, taxes and prostate exams, is inevitable, and things changed in radio. In the late '80s and early '90s, things were trending away from slick, official, ballsy-voiced men and moving toward a new "real" sound. Stripped down, nonsense-free and full of personality, radio became much more authentic, and far less *cheesy*. The voice artists for television and radio ads were more and more unconventional in their delivery and sound. A fellow Michigander named Thom Sharp made a living out of his quirky regular-guy persona on both radio and TV commercials. He was bald, bland and had a wicked midwestern accent. But he parlayed his odd charisma into a full career in television, films and stand-up comedy.

Many ad agencies fully embraced "real" in their ads, and fired their pitchmen and spokespeople in favor of more down-to-earth, everyday people: the owners, operators or employees of car dealers, electronics and furniture stores.

It was the dawn of a whole new day in broadcasting and I was right there at its outset: a young, hip, conversational personality who, like his listeners, just wanted to keep it real. There still existed, and always will, a degree of "show" in broadcasting, but the emphasis was on authenticity. Call it like you see it. Say what's on your mind. Read an ad like a person, not a "voice guy." Tell the time to listeners like you'd say it at home, "It's a quarter to eight," not "Current time: seven forty-five, fifteen minutes from the hour of eight."

At last a personality and talent were valued in the media rather than just the genetic gift of rumbling resonance. A lot of longtime career professionals found themselves struggling to fit the new mold. Many had to shift formats: leave the popular FM band and seek a news job on AM somewhere, or an oldies station where listeners could still handle their older style. In other words, it was high time for them to be themselves. Drop the vocal affectations and lighten up. Just be the person you are at home . . . with a little showmanship thrown in.

Innovative Authority

Let's change gears a little (upcoming pun intended). General Motors (there it is) opened its Saturn dealerships in 1991, right around the same time that transparency in media and advertising were all the rage. Saturn dealers and sales staff were trained, by Saturn instructors themselves, to be nice to customers, to not pressure or haggle or upsell. They should relax and let the car sell itself. It went a little something like this:

It is spring of 1991. You walk into a Saturn dealership. You're a little apprehensive. It's a whole new make of car. But you heard they were well reviewed and supposedly pretty affordable. Pretty good bang for the buck. There's one model of car, two body types: coupe or sedan. A handful of colors.

YOU: Hello?

YOUR SPOUSE (whispering): I don't think it's open.

A friendly looking, normal dude materializes in parachute pants and a Saturn polo shirt.

HIM: Hey, how's it going? I'm Steve. First time in?

YOU: Yep.

HIM: Okay. Right on. Well (gesturing), those are the cars. The price is on the window. Let me know if you want to take one for a spin. I'll be around to answer any questions you might have. And there's coffee or juice or whatever if you want to help yourself.

And that's that. He turns away and goes back to playing Tetris on his Game Boy or solving a Rubik's Cube or whatever casual thing people did in 1991.

YOU: Ummm, ohhhh-kay.

YOUR SPOUSE: Honey, is this the Gap?

There's a reason that Saturn enjoyed multiple consecutive years of customer satisfaction, sales satisfaction and high word-of-mouth sales. People loved the relaxed attitude, the real McCoy, genuine article, nonconfrontational format. Their sales style was straightforward. No haggling. It was like buying a pair of socks or a rake. This is the price. If you want the socks, pay the price. No pressure. You don't worry that the kid at Home Depot is going to take you to the cleaners because you're not very good at negotiations; he just sells you the rake. That's what Saturn did.

From the very beginning Saturn had a more genuine, people-oriented focus. Their corporate work environment was radically different from the GM mother ship's traditional plant. Saturn employees worked in teams and frontline workers sat next to managers in meetings.

Everyone's input was critical. Any employee could stop the line at any time to fix safety or quality problems on the spot. The product design phase saw designers, factory workers, engineers and outside suppliers come together for what they called simultaneous engineering. This was in sharp contrast to the traditional method of having designers come up with the idea, then "throw it over the wall" to the engineers, who did their thing, and then finally to manufacturing. They focused more on building a car that people really wanted, rather than what they themselves would like in a car. Engineering vice president Jay Wetzel put it this way: "Most great cars in history reflect the personality of one person. In our case, that person just happens to be the consumer."[1]

That consumer focus trickled all the way down to the dealerships and their "retail associates" (not salespeople). They were trained in "consultative selling," not high-pressure sales tricks. Saturn president Skip LeFauve said, "You can't just tell your retailers to be nice to people."[2]

The no-haggle, easygoing approach worked. One Saturn executive remarked, "We're not trying to sell people a car. We're helping them buy a car."[3] It was a breath of fresh air for beleaguered chumps and suckers, er, I mean car buyers. And even though Saturns were sold at full retail price, without any negotiating allowed, Saturn was number one for customer and sales satisfaction nine out of ten years. Research showed that 50 percent of Saturn customers bought primarily for the positive shopping experience, versus 25 percent for the car itself.

Let me repeat that in case you missed it. I'll write it slowly so you can take your time: half of the customers bought the car because of the *positive shopping experience,* twice as many than bought the car because they really wanted the car.

Is there a business-relevant takeaway in that for you? What would authenticity mean to your customers? Do you provide the kind of shopping experience that effectively makes your product or service secondary? Something to think about. That, and how Gary Coleman managed to remain cute well into his 40s.

Say Cheese

Most people can sniff out a phony within the first few seconds of meeting one. Among People People types, by far the most common and egregious case of fakery is when a Type I temporarily uses Type II traits to gain some advantage, rather than sincerely developing those traits and becoming an authentic Type III. When not anchored by genuine T2 values, many T1s can come off as disingenuous, deceptive and difficult to be around.

A guy I'll call "Mike White" suffered from this sickness. From the moment I met him it was clear that he had no problem socializing and chatting up strangers. He was a speaker and trainer with average skills and enjoyed being with others. A good, but not great, Type I. I don't doubt that he had Type II aspirations, but had yet to truly develop genuine warmth, concern and selflessness.

Mike's malady was what I call the "Cheese Factor" (not to be confused with the Cheesecake Factory). The guy simply could not be among other humans without adding globs of cheese to every facet of his professional life. It wasn't enough for him to just shake someone's hand and say, "Hello. I'm Mike. Pleasure to meet you." No. Mike would hold the person's hand with both of his, a few seconds longer than is typical and comfortable, pull the person closer to him, look him directly in the eye as if trying to connect to his soul, flash a huge smile and gently say, "Hi (pause, cheese grin). I'm Mike (pause, feign humility). How neat it is for me to meet you."

Ick.

Don't misunderstand. There are legitimate T2s and T3s who pull that kind of interaction off regularly and somehow manage to avoid total creepiness. Because they're honest, authentic. You know they really *do* think it's neat for them to meet you and they make you feel warm and happy. It's who they are. When it's *not* who they are, as in Mike's case, it's a two-pound block of sharp cheddar. Most people meeting Mike for the first time could immediately sniff out the lie. It was an act, pure and simple. And it went beyond greetings.

He also applied this technique in his presentations. Mike only played the part of a motivational speaker, because he lacked depth of authentic skills, either innate or learned, and the experience that informs and molds a really good speaker. Sure, people can be trained to be great presenters. They can put in the time and practice and learn how to do a good job, but even then they will strive to *be themselves*. Mike had taken a public speaking class in college and had learned the content of his speech, but so badly ached for immediate "guru" status that he figured he could just copy the gestures, vocal inflections and ponderous pacing that all the great speakers seem to do and that would be sufficient. And oh how the cheese flowed.

He would speak loud and fast, and then suddenly lower his voice as he deliberately *Punched. Each. Word.* Minutes later his face would be animated and excited as he riffed through material that made himself (and usually only himself) laugh out loud with the most delightfully whimsical chuckle. Then instantly he'd stop laughing, tilt his head a little and *whisper*—with glazed eyes focused on a distant moon just past the upper rear corner of the ceiling—some poignant, gut-wrenching moral to the story. Freeze and hold, hold, hold. Then a slow, self-satisfied, faux-humble grin to the audience . . . and . . . hold. Now a decisive spin away from the audience and a three-step march back to the podium, a reach for the reading glasses in the breast pocket of the suit jacket. Now delicately chew a stem of the glasses and look ponderous, and hold.

He was certifiable. I'm lactose intolerant as it is, but this cheese could truly do me some intestinal damage. The phony-baloney meter's needle was forever pegged in the "full-cheese" position with Mike White. His delivery and tone, whether in a hotel ballroom "motivating" managers or gathered with two or three for dinner, reminded me a bit of the world's greatest cheesebag actor, William Shatner. The stereotypical Shatner impersonations that comedians have performed over the years since *Star*

Trek are often *understated* compared to Shatner's actual performances. The beauty of Shatner, and why I admire him, is that he later recognized how awful he was and was able to parody himself and poke fun at his persona. That kind of self-awareness and authenticity provided work for him into his 80s.

I recently attended a church service where a prominent local religious leader and his wife were the invited guest speakers. She spoke first and was delightful. She had some prepared notes jotted down, but spoke from the heart as well. She was pleasant, witty and inspiring. Her message was centered on simple gospel truths and she delivered it sincerely. I was impressed.

Her husband brought no notes to the podium. He was slick, polished and professional. He oozed "preacher cheese." There was no real spirit when he spoke. Everything he said sounded like a cliché. On paper, the content of his message was probably inspiring. But his delivery was rehearsed and theatrical, filled with highs and lows and tempo changes and all manner of preacher talk. There was no real heart in it. The style distracted from the substance. He wasn't authentic. He could learn a lot from his wife.

Authenticity Is Point A

Now you may be thinking, "Isn't becoming a People Person (T3) a journey for most? As T1s and T2s learn to adopt each other's traits, as they are learning them by doing them, isn't it realistic to expect clumsy mistakes and failure? Maybe Mike White and the church speaker are just trying their hardest to become real People People."

If that's what you're thinking, congratulations, good point. If you're thinking, "What was that about Cheesecake Factory a ways back? Mmmmm, *cheesecake*," then I've lost you.

The truth is no matter where you currently find yourself in the People People spectrum you've got to have authenticity nailed. Everything else begins there. You must get back to basics. Break it down. Be who you really are to begin with. That's the launchpad. The journey to Type III isn't easy, but your desire to get there must be genuine. And what better way to develop certain attributes in yourself than to observe them in others and copy them? Replicating modeled behaviors is an effective way to adopt them, to be sure. As you read this book, at certain points you will recognize deficiencies in yourself, areas in which you feel compelled to improve for your own progress. But if you haven't yet discovered who you genuinely are, some awkwardness will accompany the effort.

The learn-by-doing method for most Type I behaviors is a fairly safe bet because they are outward expressions and physical characteristics: smiling, laughing, speaking clearly, telling jokes, meeting people, getting out in public more, attending parties, carrying on conversations, giving speeches, running meetings. These are traits that can be practiced almost immediately and, if executed poorly, represent no real danger of lasting negative impact. T2s can begin practicing T1 behaviors right away; the process may not be quick or cheap, but eventually a T3 can emerge.

On the other hand, authenticity is an absolute must for T1s to develop T2 virtues. One cannot simply mimic respect, concern, care or love and expect it to go over well with others. You can begin practicing being gracious, kind and selfless, but until they're tied to a genuine concern for others they can come off as condescending or insincere. T2s are T2s because they are that much closer to being T3s than T1s are. T1s have, I believe, a higher mountain to climb to get to T3 status. They must develop a real sense of authenticity that most T2s already possess.

The good news is the vast majority of T1s are much more authentic than they realize. Here's why: many T1s lead a double life! They suffer a split personality, and it's all of their own choosing.

Whole People

Years ago, while providing some leadership training to a group of mid-level managers at Michelin North America in Greenville, South Carolina,

I was approached by a manager who seemed upset. I had been teaching the group that they needed to lighten up, be themselves, enjoy a laugh at work and encourage it among their direct reports.

"I feel so betrayed," he said. "My boss drives me nuts."

I invited him to explain. He told me that his boss, "Lester," was a very serious, very demanding leader. He ruled with fear and discipline and extended minimal mercy to underachievers. It made it difficult for this manager to come in to work each day and he'd recently started seeking another position within the company.

"Then, the other day I'm talking with my brother Ryan," he said. "For years he's been going on about this guy he has a 'man crush' on who lives in his neighborhood. Great sense of humor, loads of laughs, life of the party. If there's a neighborhood barbecue and this guy's going, you want to be there too. Everybody wants to watch the big game at this guy's house because he's such a fun host."

"Sounds like a perfect example of someone who knows how to lighten up and enjoy life," I said.

"Yeah," he said. "I just found out that guy is Lester, my evil Jerk boss!"

I wasn't totally surprised. He continued, "What does he think—that we won't respect him? Heck, I'd respect him even more, way more than I do now! Are you kidding? It'd be great to work for a boss like that!"

Being authentic means being who you are at all times, in all places. Many Jerks and TIs at work are sweet and loving People People at home, but they keep it locked up there for fear that they'll lose respect, authority or credibility back in the office. They worry that being themselves isn't good enough, or they'll be seen as unprofessional. The authentic People Person will of course act appropriately at work, given the circumstances, but will never lose themselves entirely to their title or role.

More often than not, people identify themselves by their title and allow it to dictate how they treat others in the formal hierarchy. A People Person recognizes and respects formal authority and their position within it, but will make serious efforts to avoid becoming a Jekyll-and-Hyde duplicitous weenie. Staying grounded, not taking yourself too seriously, remembering the people at home and becoming consciously aware of the disparity between "home you" and "work you" can help on your path to constancy.

Should it really be so shocking to the system when you see your boss on Casual Friday wearing jeans and an untucked shirt like you or other "normal" people do? Why does that often seem so incongruous? Is it because you've never been able to imagine them as relaxed, casual people who do other things besides conduct high-powered meetings, chew out slackers, fuss over budgets and other formal, serious activities?

People People get it.

If they are kind, gracious, polite, forgiving, compassionate, friendly and fun with their peers and employees at work, then they know very well how critical it is to be equally or more so with their loved ones at home. And the opposite is also true. They can laugh and tell stories and just be themselves at work as they do at home. They trust that coworkers, colleagues and customers will not only accept them as the genuine article, but will truly appreciate it.

Brittanny Kreutzer, a partner at the Speaker Exchange Agency, a Kansas City–based speakers' bureau, fully embraces this holistic authenticity. She spends most of her day on the phone with clients and considers being genuine her hallmark. "I just think I'm successful at what I do because I am who I am," she said. "I put smiley faces on my e-mails and some people think that's not professional, but it's just me being me. On the phone with clients I talk about my kids and my family because I want them to know they're dealing with a *real person*."

The same is true for many politicians. Many Republican voters felt betrayed after Bob Dole lost the 1996 presidential election because Dole didn't loosen up and show his soft side until after he'd lost the race. Known for his straight-faced, monotone gravitas, Dole blew people's minds when he unleashed a wickedly funny, self-deprecating sense of humor on *The Tonight Show, The Late Show, Saturday Night Live* and other programs.

I remember thinking, "Hey, Bob, where was *that* during the campaign?" It can only be assumed that Dole's strategy was to out-serious his competitor and show America that credibility and authority wear a very grim face. Evidently America wanted a whole person as its leader, one with genuine flashes of levity, foible and imperfection.

The late, legendary entertainer George Burns once said, "In Hollywood, sincerity is everything. If you can fake that, you've got it made."

One-liners aside, sincerity is something you can't fake, at least not for the long term. People have uncanny radar for inauthenticity and, consciously or not, can spot it a mile away. Since we don't always listen to our intuition and we tend to give people the benefit of the doubt, fakers can often get away with it for a time, but not forever. Which is why, as a T1 for example, you can't remain in "T2 practice mode" too long. When Mike White ladles the dripping liquid cheese of fake concern for someone in a two-hand handshake, it doesn't for one minute feel like he's practicing a T2 value like compassion or affection. It just feels phony.

Authenticity also requires a commitment to at least strive to match actions with words. Hypocrisy is an ugly quality of the poseur. A true mensch will make every effort to practice what she preaches, even if it takes time to perfect.

There is a story about Gandhi (perhaps apocryphal, though it certainly seems to fit his character) that is a beautiful example of the power of authenticity. A woman once traveled to India to bring her son to see the famed spiritual and political leader. When they met, she said, "Sir, please tell my child not to eat sugar." The great man asked her to please return with the child the following week. Irritated and confused, she agreed and left.

A week later she returned and brought her boy to see Gandhi. Again she asked the great man to tell her son to stop eating sugar.

Gandhi tenderly looked at the boy and said, "Please don't eat sugar. It is not good for you." The boy agreed immediately, pledging that he would no longer eat sugar from that day forward. Grateful but still confused,

CHAPTER SIX

the mother said, "Why didn't you say this last week when we came? Why did you make us come back again?"

Replied Gandhi, "Last week, I too was eating sugar."[4]

Real People

Being authentic means being direct, cutting the crap. People People take a no-nonsense approach to everything they do. There's a television commercial for an energy drink that features a wild, amped-up mixed martial artist flipping and high kicking around the ring in an impressive display of athleticism. His showboating is designed to intimidate his opponent, who merely stands still in his corner watching the showy routine. At the sound of the bell, Mr. Fancy Pants immediately comes flying at his opponent with a hearty yell and a dramatic Kung Fu–style 360-degree flying kick. The other fighter calmly deflects the impact of the wild kick by catching his attacker's leg, pulls him close and knocks him out cold with one very basic punch. The commercial's tag line is "No Nonsense." It might remind you of the scene in *Raiders of the Lost Ark* when Indiana Jones handles a show-off swordsman. Unimpressed by the extraneous weapon brandishing and growing impatient, Indy merely pulls a gun and shoots the guy.

It is almost instinctual for a T1 to dress up every request, no matter how small, by using flattery or flowery words or zealously making and defending their case. This is not the nature of a T2. They will cut to the chase, using an economy of words, and thus save time and energy in getting to the answer, be it "yes" or "no." But a caution is merited: sometimes this level of authenticity (read: "frankness") isn't socially acceptable. There are times when a T2 needs to learn to exercise better T1 skills, such as tact.

When I was nineteen, I served as a Mormon missionary for two years in Spain. As a young man, unacquainted with any foreign cultures, it was an unforgettable experience. The food, the climate, the language, the history and of course the people themselves were a constant source of surprises and learning. One little quirk of the Spanish is their bluntness. I was a tall, skinny, pizza-faced adolescent with large plastic glasses, and a day didn't go by in two years without some well-meaning Spaniard reminding me of my hideous appearance.

"Madre mia, mira todos los granitos!"—"Will you look at all those zits!"

"Habra alguna crema para tu acne, no?"—"There must be some kind of zit cream, isn't there?"

There's a limit on straightforwardness that shouldn't be breached, even in the spirit of full, colorful honesty and authenticity. Telling a self-conscious teenager that his face looks like the ceiling of a planetarium is beyond the breach. Nevertheless, I had been raised in a pretty laid-back environment, where family and friends really didn't put too much stock in temporary deformities like pimples. I could handle a few awkward social customs for a couple of years. I'd grown up with people that accepted who and how they were and afforded me the same courtesy. I've always appreciated genuine, down-to-earth associates.

SIX People

There's a musical act in Branson, Missouri, called SIX. The original name was Six Real Brothers, aka Barry, Kevin, Lynn, Jak, Owen and Curtis Knudsen. They shortened the name because, well, it sounded cooler. But the fact is these real brothers are cooler than most other acts in their industry.

They have been singing together since they were in grade school. Their mother had the voice; their father the ear. He taught them to harmonize and they garnered some notoriety at national barbershop competitions. They were young, cute and talented. They were invited to perform on the *Donny & Marie* show in the '70s, where they made several appearances, a sort of giving back gesture on the Osmonds' part for the exposure Andy Williams had given them on his show in the early '60s.

Jak and I were close friends in junior high and high school, and I got to know the other brothers very well. I remember hanging out in their tiny wooden house and being forever amazed how they (and four younger brothers; if you're keeping track, that's ten boys!) all managed to get along. They must have slept at least three to a bedroom, plus they had one entire room just for music and singing.

What everyone loved about them back then is the same thing that thousands love about them today. They were all very down to earth. There was no pretense, no conceit, no putting on airs. They were a pretty big deal once we all saw them perform on national television with the Osmonds. But, if anything, they were obsessive about being "normal." They shared a certain quirky sense of humor about their less-than-ideal economic situation, but discovered real joy and security in being honest, decent, fun-loving (if not hell-raising) boys.

It was always Joyce Knudsen's dream that all ten of her sons would go serve as missionaries for the church. This selfless, volunteer effort is a huge time and financial commitment, not only for a young man or woman, especially one whose sights are set on stardom, but also for his or her family. Nevertheless, all six of the singing brothers, one by one around age nineteen, took a two-year hiatus from the act to go across the world to be missionaries. The group rolled with the decade-long personnel changes while moving first to Los Angeles, then to Phoenix and later to Las Vegas to pursue their entertainment careers. With the four youngest boys still living at home, Joyce died of a brain tumor. Within a few years the rest of the ten brothers also served missions, fulfilling their mother's wish.

The six Knudsen singers finally settled their families in Branson in 2007. Curtis, the youngest of the group, said, "Branson is all about family and God. It just seemed to be the perfect fit for us."

Their show is the hands-down fan favorite and an absolute must-see year in and year out (Best New Show, 2007; Best Show, 2008, 2009). Audiences adore these immensely talented brothers whose voices blend in perfect harmonies in a fast-paced, colorful stage show that showcases their humor and fun.

Whenever I'm in the area, I stop in and say hello. They are still accessible, humble and down to earth; legions of fans return annually like swallows to Capistrano to see them again and again. They are outgoing, affable and extremely talented. The Knudsens learned at a young age to embrace who they are, to develop their talents while they developed their own unique personalities, combining the two for a success and happiness they could only dream of as young brothers learning their craft.

CHAPTER SEVEN
People People and Respect

Respect is the core attribute of the Type II People Person. It embodies the real spirit of CARE that People People possess. In fact, this principle could be called care, concern, compassion, kindness, generosity . . . even, yep, love. Respect encompasses selfless service, patience, warmth and appreciation.

Sharing People (Literally)

As I mentioned in Chapter Four, it is one thing for a company to care for its people. It is quite another when the people really care for each other. Scottrade is an online investment company with 3,200 employees that also happened to make the 2012 Best Companies to Work For list (No. 31). Scottrade associates have a lot in common, but few are connected quite like two of them in Billings, Montana, who now share a liver.

In July 2011, senior stockbroker Christine Mueller donated 30 percent of her liver to Nicole Bykonen, a former financial office assistant in her branch. Before the transplant, Nicole had been given one year to live. Today she's back home raising her three kids and has normal liver function for the first time in seven years. Her donor, Christine, is considered the fastest-healing liver donor ever seen at the Mayo Clinic.

The two had worked together in Scottrade's Billings branch for a year, during which Nicole was severely ill with colon, thyroid and liver problems. One day, Christine nonchalantly made Nicole an extraordinary offer: if Nicole needed a liver, she'd donate.

"I once saw a TV show about organ donation," Christine said, "and I told myself, 'If I'm ever in this situation, I'll definitely donate to help a friend.'"

The human liver is the only internal organ that can naturally regenerate lost tissue, so a living person can safely donate and expect to return to full function. Little did Nicole know she'd soon need to accept Christine's offer. Nicole endured a series of misdiagnoses before leaving Scottrade on disability in June 2010, and in February 2011 she was diagnosed with a rare autoimmune disorder that damages and blocks bile ducts inside and outside the liver. In Nicole's case, the disease caused bile duct cancer.

Nicole's time was running out. She had already undergone chemotherapy and radiation, and now her only hope was a new liver. The waiting period for a liver from a deceased donor was two years, and her doctors said she'd need one within six months to survive.

So Nicole called Christine and asked, "Remember when you offered to donate your liver? Would you really do that?"

Christine didn't think twice. "Within an hour I was on the phone with the Mayo Clinic," she said, and the two underwent the transplant in July.

And it saved Nicole's life.

"It was an easy decision," Christine said. "The whole time, I was thinking, 'This could be me.' I'm lucky enough to be healthy, and I want to share that."

Christine had no fear of the surgery, the long recovery or the potential complications that could follow. But the cost of losing pay for the five weeks she would be out weighed on her. That was until she spoke with Scottrade's Human Resources Department and received the gift of thirty extra sick days (six weeks) to recover.

Christine credits Scottrade's generosity with helping her maintain the positive attitude that doctors believe caused her speedy recovery. And the optimism has stuck with Christine ever since, as she's watched her story encourage countless others to take risks to help others.

"If I worked for any other company, the transplant would have been a lot harder—or impossible," Christine said.

Maybe. The company itself can only do so much. In this case, they helped set the stage that allowed the surgery to happen. But it took an incredibly selfless gesture by a single person to save Nicole's life. At the end of the day, individual human beings are the engine that drives respect through a company, even one that respects its people like Scottrade does.

Because "respect" encompasses so much, it's simpler to break it down into three basic ideas: latitude, attitude and gratitude.

Latitude

People People are quick to forgive and forget. They recognize the innately imperfect state of all people. So they'll let go of grudges and allow latitude for others' mistakes.

They are patient with others' choices and styles at work, home and in public. They don't micromanage; they give others flexibility and freedom to make decisions, use judgment and take action. People People possess the perspective needed to fully tolerate behaviors and opinions that differ from their own. If trust is the be-all and end-all of great places to work, then latitude is critical to bosses and coworkers alike.

But don't be fooled. Latitude may sound like a simple enough concept, but it will stretch most leaders' commitment to the People People cause.

Particularly in the workplace, latitude means allowing others to be who they are, to do what makes them happy, to work in a style that best suits them. The culture must remain a constant, but how individuals contribute to it often results in an exercise in tolerance for leaders at any level.

No matter how jealously company managers protect the culture by making sure only the right people are hired, a few bogies will sneak through. That's a given. They will need to be onboarded, indoctrinated, socialized and sniffed out as soon as possible, then dealt with accordingly (change 'em or chuck 'em), before they can do much harm. But what about all the right ones you've hired? The ones that pass the culture test? They may not be bad apples, but they are certainly not cookie-cutter, homogenous robots that goose-step in formation, either. Each will bring his or her own set of personality disorders, work philosophies, bizarre ideas and cubicle decorations to your cherished workplace. They may work in a way that generally supports the mission, vision and values of the organization, but no two will carry it out exactly the same, much less as precisely prescribed by the company documents HR has distributed.

As a People Person you must allow for such disparities among the ranks. It's the diversity of backgrounds, experiences, education and favored methods that make a powerful team. You know that synergy is real. Latitude means you trust the choices you've made in discovering the right talent. And then you trust the talent.

Workplace flexibility is a good test of that trust. These days, most caring companies (and many that aren't, but are willing to acknowledge the need) offer a broad menu of flex-work options that typically include latitude in work schedules, hours, time-off programs, overtime, leaving early, and working from home or elsewhere. Smart employers won't use a one-size-fits-all approach in implementing a flexibility strategy. They strive for a more custom fit, depending on the person and her specific job. If she were a bus driver, for example, offering her a telecommuting option doesn't make sense.

Research shows strong evidence that when companies find the right flexibility fit for their people there is higher employee engagement, a lower employee perception of work overload, better employee physical and mental health and greater employee satisfaction with the work/life balance.[1] It wouldn't take the average primate more than a couple of seconds to deduce the benefits to an organization's health.

There is no more extreme example of that level of latitude than a Results-Only Work Environment (ROWE).[2] This polarized model of work/life balance and flexibility gives 100 percent freedom to employees to do whatever they please with their time, to never have to come into work if they don't want to, to attend a school play, go shopping, even take an afternoon nap in a backyard hammock—as long as they produce agreed-upon results.

Now that's some latitude.

While some organizations might find themselves in a position to board up their corporate offices and let everyone work from the privacy of their cushy domestic lairs (in their underwear, naturally), the majority of businesses still require the regular human touch to get things devised, developed and delivered. But there is something to be said about the ROWE plan; by taking it to the absolute extreme it has made the argument for less-radical flexibility options that much easier to make.

The point is that as a People Person, you would be far more likely to extend latitude to your coworkers or direct reports regarding their attendance at work, their scheduled hours or if they break away to attend a child's (ideally their own) gymnastics meet. There are far too many busybodies and bootlickers wasting precious time worrying themselves silly over how long Pamela spent at lunch or why Corbin didn't come in this morning until 9:15! With clear communication, an individual worker's expected output or results can be agreed upon. These then serve as an accountability measure. The employee is offered latitude (trust) to accomplish the results however they choose. In other words, "Do your job well. That's what we pay you for. We don't want you to feel bad for attending a family function, a doctor's appointment or an afternoon matinee with your kids, or for taking a three-day weekend, because you're not worth squat on Fridays anyway. You've got a cell phone and a laptop, and if we absolutely need something from you, we know how to reach you. We don't need to see you every single day. If this level of freedom is difficult for you and you need more structure to truly thrive, then we'll adjust. If results don't happen, we will adjust anyway."

I don't *know* that I have attention deficit disorder. I've never been diagnosed. I do think a few rounds with some kind of therapist would probably be really good for me, but up until now I've managed just fine without knowing what I "have." But I do know that I cannot come into my office, sit down at the computer and write straight through until lunch. I usually have six or seven different programs open and am working on travel plans, contracts, marketing information, conference calls and occasionally rehearsing a role (I still do the occasional commercial or TV episode) all at the same time as I labor over the next eleven words of this book. My close friend and associate Adrian Gostick would have had this book written in a fortnight, during his smoke breaks (he doesn't smoke). I've fathered three children since I began this *chapter*. He can stay riveted on his task until it's complete or at least until it's time to go home. I don't rivet. I'm not even sure I know what a rivet looks like. I tend to procrastinate. I work better under pressure. I think a ticking clock brings out the best in me. I don't particularly care for the stress and anxiety my disorder brings, but I haven't fixed it yet. Until I do, I can be counted on to deliver great work, on time. Past employers have graciously overlooked my frustrating modus operandi and extended me latitude in this regard because the end product left little or nothing wanting.

Some people work well with music playing. Others demand complete silence. Some furrow their brows at the slightest hint of frivolity. Others play office soccer with balls of duct tape. People People show respect for others' senses of humor and play or total lack of either. For most People People, but not all, a spirit of joviality and jocularity comes naturally, so extending latitude to the lighthearted isn't a difficulty. But all too often the opposite also occurs: extroverts complain that so-and-so is a real stick in the mud or a killjoy, and consequently doesn't really fit with the team. A People Person extends latitude in all directions, not just where it best aligns with her own interests.

In terms of fun at work, latitude is what you allow others to get away with, what you tolerate or permit without complaining to upper management or getting into arguments. Being a People Person means caring more *about* other people and less about what other people *do*.

Attitude

If latitude is showing respect to others by extending them the courtesy to be who they are and do what they do, attitude is what and how *you* are, or what others allow *you* to get away with. What is your preferred work style? Do you like to have fun at work or keep things serious? What about in your private life? Is your attitude in everyday situations consistent with your People Person image at work?

If People People respect others, it's a product of their attitude. This attitude must remain the same at work, at home and in public. How well does your public attitude show respect to others?

How about **in traffic,** for instance? (You knew this would eventually find its way into a book about People People, didn't you?) For a bit of context, as I write this I am staring out my rather large hotel room window overlooking Plaza de España in Barcelona, a wonderfully massive traffic roundabout with six major traffic arteries all converging in a state of surprising efficiency.

A moment ago, however, one of the million black and yellow (like bumblebees) taxis made a bold (and legal) move that upset a passenger in the car that got cut off, prompting the passenger to flash an angry gesture. Apparently not satisfied that his curse word and accompanying sign language were received by the cabbie, he decided to up the ante and hurl a liter bottle of water at the cab, bouncing it off the back window and nearly taking out an innocent scooterist. Feel better, amigo?

Answer truthfully these questions about your attitude when you drive, if you dare:

> Do you think of driving as a competitive sport? (And I don't mean the Indy 500 or Laguna Seca.)
>
> Do you frequently run late and need to speed or drive recklessly to make up time?
>
> Do you make obscene gestures at other drivers or honk obnoxiously?
>
> If someone cuts you off in traffic, do you catch up to them and respond in kind?
>
> Do you drive in the left (or passing) lane even when you're not passing someone?
>
> Do you tailgate others to get them to speed up or move out of your way?

If you answered "yes" to *any* of these questions, that's pretty normal. It doesn't make you a total Jerk. You haven't disqualified yourself as a People Person; you have some work to do, but who doesn't? But if you answered "yes" to *all* of these questions, you probably need to have your driver's license suspended for a season while you sequester yourself in an oxygen-rich sensory deprivation tank to rediscover the meaning of life.

Fully one-half of drivers who are subjected to aggressive driving behavior on the road respond with aggression of their own, thus risking a more serious confrontation. According to a recently released national survey, when a driver gets the finger, is cut off or tailgated, 50 percent of the victims respond with horn honking, yelling, cutting off and obscene gestures of their own.

The survey revealed that 34 percent of drivers say they honk their horn at the aggressor, 27 percent yell, 19 percent give the finger back, 17 percent flash their headlights, and 7 percent mimic the initial aggressive driving behavior. Two percent of drivers admit to trying to run the aggressor off the road.[3] And of course the occasional Spaniard hurls water bottles.

People People have the good sense to know that others' bad driving is not intended as a personal offense. Most people don't care about you at all on the road. They're busy yammering with a passenger or on a phone call, talking to themselves, deep in thought, singing along with the Killers at the top of their lungs or just plain fast asleep at the wheel. In any case, you're just another obstacle in their way. A People Person respects drivers of all abilities and does his best to keep himself, his passengers and other motorists safe by being courteous, patient and calm. Like a Boy Scout in a Buick.

How are you **at sporting events**? Having raised five sons, I've attended my share of Little League baseball, football, soccer, basketball and wrestling competitions. There is no limit to the idiotic things parents will say and do when cheering for their kid and her team. People People love and support their children, naturally, but somehow manage to do it without pulling a gun and holding it to the head of the football coach of a team of six- and seven-year-olds because their son isn't getting enough playing time (true story). A respectful attitude means letting the coaches coach and the players play. People People cheer for good effort, good sportsmanship and good offense or defense from either team. They relax and enjoy the fact that their kid is learning discipline, developing confidence, making new friends and doing it in a nonvirtual setting with other human beings.

One of my sons, Matt, was rather tall as a nine-year-old so he started playing basketball. Because of his size, they made him a post player and he was very good. He was fast, strong and an amazing jumper. We had high aspirations for him and were thrilled that as he got older he made it onto a club team. Graduating from an "everyone plays" league to a club team also meant being forced to put up with weenie parents who were convinced their son was the next LeBron James. This ratcheted up the audience Jerk-o-Meter enough that my wife and I grew weary of attending games. In a bittersweet twist of natural evolution, my son pretty much had grown to full height by the age of thirteen, standing a not-so-towering 5 feet 11 inches. Not a short kid, but nowhere near tall enough to play down low. Not having learned enough ballhandling, passing and shooting skills to play as a guard or small forward, he quickly fell into no-man's-land and decided to give up the sport.

We were anything but heartbroken. We never harbored NBA dreams or expectations. We just knew he was happy playing. Now he finds happiness playing the piano. He is a gifted young talent; he's never taken a lesson but can sit and play brilliantly improvised pieces for hours and hours. Plus, whenever he wants to he can still play ball recreationally (and totally dominate!).

People People also respect others when attending professional or collegiate sporting events. They sit in the actual seats that correspond to their purchased tickets, thus avoiding all of the fussing and worrying and stress and conflict that the rest of us feel when some inconsiderate group of jackasses improvise seating arrangements so that they can sit together. A few years ago while visiting Seville, Spain, to speak at the annual meeting of the International Association of Amusement Parks and Attractions (Motto: Vomiting is the Universal Language!), I had the chance to attend a *futbol* (soccer) match between Sevilla and Real Betis. I absolutely love La Liga (the premier Spanish soccer league), and was able to purchase a ticket from the hotel concierge desk (one hundred euros, if you must know the cost). The concierge assured me I was paying for a very good seat, just eight rows up from the field. He said this would be a great game since the teams are rivals.

Little did I know!

Both teams are based in Seville. An intra-city rivalry. Bloods versus Crips, but slightly less carnage. The place was beyond jam-packed. There were large groups of ticketless hooligans outside the stadium running in packs trying to break down the gates and overtake the security guards in an effort to—what?—see the game from a portal?

When I flashed my ticket to a guard, he quickly rushed me to a secret entrance and slammed shut the door behind me just as the mob rushed up. They banged and yelled. I half expected a felled tree hoisted by angry villagers to batter down the door. After several minutes of trying to orient myself, I finally found my seat. But it was already taken . . . and then some. There must have been twenty-five people, all standing, in my row of fifteen seats. I ended up standing in an aisle about ten feet behind my seat the entire game.

Respect for audience members includes using event-appropriate tone and language. How sad it is to get settled in with your kids for a game only to have the swearing and yelling at the refs, the other team and its fans start up even before kickoff. A People Person somehow is able to restrain himself from karate chopping the Jerk behind him in the throat, but will likely need the gentle intervention of family members to help.

On public transportation, are you cordial and polite? Do you regularly give up your seat for the disabled and elderly? People People hold the door for others, scoot over, hold their bag or purse in their lap rather than give it its own seat. They fill in the empty spaces in the back that the people boarding a crowded bus or train can't see, making more room so that no one's left standing on the curb or waiting for the next shuttle.

They respect others' private space. They don't read books, newspapers, magazines or text messages over someone's shoulder. A People Person has previously determined how many volume clicks on his iPod is just loud enough for him to hear "Funky Cold Medina" on his headphones over the sounds of the subway, without every other passenger being subject to the throbbing, tinny, distorted fuzz. Intoxicated People People, even in their haze, will have already made the decision long ago to just stay off public transportation entirely. For heaven's sake, spare us all and take a cab.

People People can monitor and regulate the volume of the conversations they're having on buses, subways, trams and trains. It doesn't require a polo mallet to the temple for them to recognize that literally no one else wants to hear about how their boyfriend was a total Jerk on their trip to Paris and how he tweeted a photo of a hot French chick that he said looked just like Halle Berry, but he doesn't think Halle Berry's hot or anything, he just thought it was like a "separated at birth" thing, but he totally ticked me off anyway and then *look!* he bought me this awesome watch, isn't it cute?

Traveling abroad? Do you grow frustrated at the thoughtlessness of Japanese subway conductors who only announce the stops in Japanese? Have you ever been served dinner in a French restaurant—literally in France—and laughed aloud at the portion size? "Ha ha. Come on; bring out the actual entrée!" And above all, do you *stand* on the moving *walkway* at airports? The list of traveler offenses stemming from a poor attitude is infinite and ever increasing.

A People Person doesn't take a vacation from being a People Person. They are that way whether they're crammed armpit deep on a Mexican microbus or tucked under expensive high-thread-count sheets in their lounge-level suite at the JW Marriott. People first, always and anywhere.

At movie theaters—two words: Shut. Up.

At work—a positive and supporting attitude to a boss or team leader is a powerful show of respect at work. Deferring to another's judgment, decision, idea or suggestion does not always come easy, particularly when the other person is a peer and rival. In a competitive and often cutthroat corporate culture, where promotions are scarce and raises are rare, every edge you can secure over the competition is essential. Even a People Person knows this, but integrity and respect for others influences their attitude toward coworkers and associates. People People may not necessarily agree with everything their director (who may have been a former peer) develops and implements, they may even express their objections in an appropriate forum, but they will not run a negative campaign to impeach the director or deliberately and underhandedly attempt to undermine her efforts.

People People are genuinely happy for others' successes and wins. The late Stephen Covey emphasized that there is an infinite amount of glory, praise and credit to be had. Just because someone else receives applause for outstanding work, it in no way diminishes the amount of applause you might receive. There are enough accolades for everyone. Maintaining the attitude that any praise is good praise, even if it's for someone else on your team, is a healthy perspective. What benefits one benefits all. A People Person may spend an instant or a lifetime developing this attitude. Either way, it's the right direction to be headed.

Gratitude

Before he retired in September 2012, Howard Cooper decided to thank his employees at Howard Cooper Import Center in a special way for their service over the past forty-seven years. The Ann Arbor, Michigan, car dealer presented checks to each of his eighty-nine employees in the amount of $1,000 for every year they worked for him. The driver of the parts van was handed a check for $28,000. A mechanic got one for $26,000. "I wanted to thank my employees and that was a way I could do it," Cooper said. "I hope it makes a difference in their lives like they have made in mine."[4]

If you have any intention of becoming a People Person, learning to be grateful is not only fundamental, but perhaps the quickest route to getting there. You can start thanking people immediately, without any grandiose gestures like Cooper's. Thanking others is an attribute that is common to both T1s and T2s, but more frequent among T2s. Since it is difficult to truly express appreciation without a minimum level of sincerity, T1s often seem lacking in genuine gratitude. The mere expression of thanks is torpedoed by the absence of legitimate appreciation. Comedian Steve Martin demonstrated the meaninglessness of rapid-fire, perfunctory thanks in his comedy act in the early '70s. At the close of his live routine he'd look out at the audience packed into a concert hall or comedy club and say, "You've been great, really. I want to thank each and every one of you for coming by: Thank you. Thank you. Thank you. Thank you. Thank you. Thank you. Thank you. . . ." And on and on he went for a minute or more as fast as he could.

Gratitude is twofold: expressing gratitude to others, and possessing a general sense of gratitude. In the case of the latter, gratitude is a state of mind that defines many People People. It is the fundamental principle of perspective that informs their mood, actions and outlook. A feeling of gratitude allows them to enjoy the ride. We'll talk more about that type of gratitude in Chapter Nine.

Thanking People

Gratitude as expressed to others in a work context through appreciative words, actions, symbols and tangible tokens like gifts or awards is the most effective way to show respect. In short, saying thanks really matters in business. More so than latitude and attitude, gratitude is a direct, demonstrable application of People People principles.

People People at work employ this tool both instinctively and deliberately. Gratitude at work is most commonly referred to as "employee recognition," and believe me it requires a lot more than a plaque for "Accounting Supervisor of the Year, Dubuque Southeast" given out at the annual company banquet to truly communicate real gratitude, the gratitude that reinforces respect. It may be enough for the *organization* to limit itself to appreciating its employees every five years with a ring or a watch or golf clubs, but employees need more from their *boss* and *peers*. And I don't mean more *stuff*. Nobody can afford to present stainless steel serving platters and crystal paperweights every time they feel the urge to appreciate someone. People need more of the day-to-day recognition experiences. For many organizations, that requires a complete culture overhaul; for others, just some tweaks and adjustments.

"While we've always been good to our people, we've become even better at it in the past seven or eight years," Maureen Wolfe, senior vice president/director of human resources at ESL Federal Credit Union in

Rochester, New York, told me. "That's because as we've grown in the past decade we have recognized the increased value of putting our people first—and the competitive advantage it brings. We have dramatically increased the attention we pay to such areas as . . . recognition . . . and fun in the workplace . . . to increase engagement and enhance the overall employee experience."

Wolfe and Martial Bednar, an employee communications manager, agree that the real turning point in their cultural revolution was the official launch of their new employee recognition program, which focuses on acknowledging the day-to-day contributions (as well as the long-term, higher-impact accomplishments) of all of ESL's employees.

"We committed to creating a 'thriving culture of recognition' at ESL," said Bednar. "It vividly demonstrates our commitment to people."

It should be no surprise that when I asked where this People People spirit had its genesis Wolfe and Bednar enthusiastically identified their CEO, Dave Fiedler.

"Dave is a rarity among CEOs, a *real* People Person," Bednar told me. "He is incredibly friendly and approachable, with a down-to-earth warmth and self-effacing humor that draws people in—whether it's a senior vice president, a teller or a member."

Incidentally, ESL Federal Credit Union was among the 50 Best Small Companies to Work For in America for 2010 and 2011, and, more importantly, Wolfe said, "Despite the state of the overall economy of the past few years, ESL has had some of its most profitable years ever!"

Gratitude Basics

The concept of gratitude isn't too tough to grasp. It's something most people learned from childhood: say "thank you." It was part of the whole "mind your Ps and Qs" conversation. I still have no idea what Ps and Qs actually are, but embedded in there somewhere was the notion to be thankful to people. Primary school teachers are also quite influential in teaching young students to say "please" and "thank you."

Below is the text from a thank you note that worked its way around the Web. The scanned image was of a handwritten thank you letter on fat-lined paper from a fourth-grade boy named Flint to Texas meteorologist Albert Ramon, who had visited the boy's class. Undoubtedly, after Ramon's exit, the teacher had everyone "take out a sheet of paper and a number two pencil and write Mr. Ramon a letter to thank him for coming all the way here and honoring us with his visit." Imagine the fourth-grader's handwriting in block letter pencil, including punctuation and spelling errors:

Dear mr. Ramon,

Thank you for coming to our school and teaching us about weather.
Some day when I become supreme Ultra-Lord of the universe I will not make you a slave, you will live in my 200 story castle where unicorn servants will feed you doughnuts off their horns.
I will personally make you a throne that is half platnum and half solid gold and jewel encrested.
Thank you again for teaching us about meteoriligy, you're more awesome than a monkey wearing a tuxedo made out bacon riding a cyborg unicorn with a lightsaber for the horn on the tip of a Space Shuttle closing in on Mars while ingulfed in flames . . . And in case you didn't know, that's pretty dang sweet.

Sincerely, Flint.

If you'll recall the not-so-flattering comments from employees of a large retailer in Chapter Five, a few of them touched on this issue of recognition, validation, appreciation and giving credit where credit is due. In fact, in the past two decades I have visited over a thousand companies, large and small, domestic and international, great places and lousy places, and a lack of sincere appreciation from management is far and away the number one biggest complaint among employees.

Too many leaders rely solely on the company to take care of recognition and rewards. They figure their top job is to tell people what to do and how to do it, and then make sure that they do it. Somebody else can make sure they get paid or receive rewards for their work, they reason. "I'm not here for anybody to like me; I'm not their babysitter or their best friend. I'm not their therapist or confessor." Harrumph, grumble, grumble, grumble.

There is such a staggering amount of research available on the motivating effect of "carrot" (as opposed to "stick") managers that I will refrain from bombarding you with what should be, by now, old news to you. My colleagues at The Culture Works, Chester Elton and Adrian Gostick, have effectively added a new genre of business books to this topic, canonized as must-reads for the budding People Person. Their Carrot series, to which I contributed (*The Carrot Principle, A Carrot a Day, The 24-Carrot Manager, The Daily Carrot Principle*), are reference guides to aspiring people leaders at all levels.

So, in the spirit of nonbombardment, I will merely share the most important truths about gratitude at work for those of you who don't typically read any books by authors with an initial in their name or who wear glasses in the dust jacket photograph:

1. Gratitude for peers' and employees' accomplishments is the number one overall action you can take to drive employee engagement. Recognition must be sincere and timely and include relevant specific details about the employee's actions or behavior. People People are hardwired to look for and point out the good things their associates accomplish.

2. Work cultures where appreciation is most frequent and sincere enjoy the highest levels of employee retention. Many people will turn down more money to stay with People People who respect them by expressing frequent praise and acknowledgment.

3. Companies where employees rate "employee recognition" highest dramatically outperform competitors where gratitude is infrequent or done poorly.

I'm Not Saying It's Easy

Respect is about being good to people. It demands a conscious choice for most of us. As we work on respecting others' points of view, likes and dislikes, styles of clothing, work habits and, perhaps most challenging, choice of baby names, we begin to—Wait. Wait. Stop.

I have to address this. What in the world are some parents smoking? This is an area that requires a lot of work for me. Let's be honest: some people are just stupid. Now that may sound harsh, but in the spirit of full disclosure I have openly admitted that I'm striving to become a People Person myself, so I'm allowed a moment of weak judgmentalism. I literally have to muster every ounce of energy to contort my facial muscles into a semiauthentic looking smile and summon what must be the lamest-sounding fake voice of approval when new parents tell me their adorable infant is named "Blueberry" or "Copper" or "Phineas Corkle" or some character from an obscure piece of teen literature.

"Ooooh, *Poughkeepsie,* how adorable!"

"Yeah. We're calling him Kip for short."

Yikes.

Indeed, learning to fully become respectful of others is a lofty goal for some of us. But it's part and parcel of a People People revolution, individually or collectively. Through competitive compensation and benefits, flexible work options, comfortable physical environments and other cool intangibles, an organization respects its people. It's then the responsibility of people like you and me to show respect on an individual level. Applying latitude, attitude and gratitude regularly is key to becoming an authentic People Person.

By definition, a People Person doesn't have to engage a total stranger in conversation at a ball game, bus stop or nightclub. The concept of effective communication from a true people perspective goes beyond the standard situations of sales presentations, job interviews or interacting with a customer. Most People People are experts in those situations anyway, but don't be fooled. We all know people who can put on their people persona and become the belle of the ball, but later disparage the very crowd they chummed with. Who hasn't been surprised to see a charismatic coworker with renowned people skills treat his family like crap at the company picnic or push others out of the way to be the first in line at the barbecue? Embracing a people mentality and attitude means being authentic, sincere, gracious and warm in all phases of business and life. A real People Person cares.

Connecting with Individuals

And because they care, People People are careful to make sure comprehension of message is accomplished. They put some effort into their conversations. They want the message to get through; a bewildered or bored look from the receiver is highly undesirable, so a People Person tries hard to be clear.

Of course, not every situation requires a concentrated effort to communicate on a deeper level. "Can you please pass the split peas pie?" is a simple request that requires no major people skills beyond common courtesy in asking politely and saying "please," and is unlikely to have much impact on the receiver beyond making him or her exert a tiny amount of physical effort. (Incidentally, a People Person will utterly refuse to pass split peas pie to anyone on the grounds that it tastes really nasty.)

Because People People care, they are concerned with *how* a message is received—if it's perceived correctly. Simple reception of a message can be instantly verified by observation.

For example:

"Tickets, please," the conductor says, peering down at you, his hole punch poised for action. Your response is to hand over your ticket. Nothing more needs to be said. The conductor needs no more evidence that his message was received.

"Tickets, please," you mumble through the round, metallic grate of the Cineplex bulletproof window. Brianna, the pizza-faced (I can mock; I've earned the right) adolescent cashier, without making eye contact, says, "For what?"

Well, for a movie. Duh.

But the fact is, you have to specify which movie, which showing of the movie, how many tickets and if you are a student, a senior citizen or a member of the Frequent Filmgoers Club, which after twenty purchases, or the equivalent of renting a Learjet for a weekend, you get 5 percent off your ticket *and* a free Sour Patch Kid (singular). Besides, you can't just *mumble* into a ticket booth grate. You have to produce some real volume for your voice to snake its way through those filters; push from the abdomen.

A People Person *tries harder* in their communication to:

Be Honest. Honest communication is tricky business. If you commit to full disclosure of truths and wide-open, blatant sincerity you will inevitably cause grief, pain and discomfort to others and yourself. A true People Person will carefully consider this before rigidly adhering to 100 percent honesty. Care for others is their focus and it will determine to what degree communication will be honest.

People People can be trusted to handle difficult and sensitive situations such as breaking bad news, letting someone down easy and owning up to mistakes. Because they are known to genuinely have concern for others, disappointing news and somewhat less than positive messages aren't as stressful or confrontational as they might otherwise be.

Listen. It wouldn't be a stretch for most to consider listening as one of humankind's greatest challenges. Many of us are so self-centered that we cannot listen to someone for longer than a few seconds without becoming distracted by our own thoughts, or worse, interrupting the other person. A study done with a group of doctors bore this out. Doctors were asked how long they figured they listened to their patients without interrupting. The average answer was around three minutes. After observing the doctors with their patients over a period of time, the actual average amount of time the doctors listened without interrupting was 20 seconds.[1] Okay, we reason, so what? A doctor needs to interject to better understand the symptoms and diagnose the problems. And we likely feel the need to do the same. To better understand the conversation, we interrupt it and add our own input, which shapes and guides the flow. People People make an effort to really listen. The best ones actually care about what the other person is saying; it's not just pretend. Even when the content is somewhat banal, active listening is a hallmark of real People People.

Be Interesting. People People are interesting to talk to. They may not possess the wittiest humor, the most pleasant speaking voice, or share wild tales of adventure, but they abhor tedium. Content need not be exclusively humorous or entertaining, but the manner of speech, the smile in the voice and the twinkle in the eye is characteristic. They care that their audience—from one person to a packed Turkish bath—is interested, entertained and enlightened. And so should you.

Be Authentic. See the story about "Mike White" in Chapter Six and do the complete opposite.

Be Polite. People People speak clearly and at a volume that is appropriate for the setting. You rarely have to strain to hear every word from a People Person, unless of course they're laryngitic, have a mouthful of Cinnabon or only know seven words in your language. (Yes, those are the only three extant scenarios.)

Keeping conversational content polite is another area where People People try harder. They try to use proper grammar and socially acceptable words and phrases. They concede points and admit errors. They answer direct questions directly. They maintain an appropriately comfortable distance. They make an effort to slow down when talking to someone who is learning their language. When speaking a foreign language themselves, they will attempt to speak slowly and as clearly as possible, careful to pronounce words with as much of the local accent as they are able to.

Public Communications

In a presentation setting, a People Person recognizes the inherent obligation he has to reciprocate value for the audience's attention. In short, he needs to *pay* them to listen and comprehend. If this concept sounds strange to you, that's okay. That's the point of the book: to help you understand and assess areas where you may be lacking in people skills.

You've been asked to deliver a presentation to a group of potential clients who are interested in your company's new offering of accounting software. Your first reaction is panic coupled with a foreboding sense of doom. You hate being in front of people, you stutter and stammer when you get nervous and a *lot* is riding on the flawless execution of your pitch. After a couple of sleepless nights and a few uncontrollable fits, shakes and spasms of stress, you remember that your product is amazing and will stand on its own and that all you have to do is turn it on for them and get out of the way while you walk them through a demo. Wrong.

A People Person sees this as an exciting opportunity to get to know more people. She will first focus on making some kind of connection with her audience in an authentic way. Maybe she will be a little nervous anyway, so she'll just admit, "I'm a little nervous—we really do have an amazing product here and I just want to make sure you all get a good chance to see what it can do. I hope I can answer whatever questions you'll have as we talk through this." She takes comfort in the knowledge that this is *her* presentation and no one has any idea what she'll say or do or what might be constituted as a mistake. In a perfect world, some of her audience members—these VIP clients—are People People too, and they are pulling for her to do a good job as well. She'll wisely ask her audience members little questions to break the ice: "How far did you guys come to be here? Who had the longest flight?" She may share a brief anecdote about her one trip to Hong Kong and how impressed she was by its natural beauty. In short, she will connect with her audience on a people level first. She will speak from the heart, off the cuff and eye to eye. Prepared, to be sure. But not programmed. She must win them over, if even a little. For even the smallest of reasons, they must *like* her. They're not interested in smoke and mirrors, they just want to hear the facts, see the product and have a good time.

An effective presentation or speech, in any setting, will strive to be a good time. In fact, can you think of any scenario or situation where you would *not want* to have a good time? Since it's all relative, it's a safe bet that everyone, everywhere, at any time is hoping to have a good time no matter what they're doing. A People Person zeros in on this immediately. The trite query "Is everybody having a good time?" is not only annoyingly tacky, but wholly unnecessary. A great presenter, a People Person, will read the mood and expressions of the audience in their eyes, body language and expressions. People People make this their objective, to ensure that others are comfortable and content. The broader message is almost secondary in importance, if not completely dependent on the comfort and contentment of the audience, for the message won't be received well, if at all, if the mood is wrong. Don't get caught up in the notion that content trumps performance. It doesn't. Content is part of the performance, a really, really important part to be sure.

Just for fun, here is a list of places and situations where people are not expecting, but are really hoping, to have a good time, and how People People communication skills can make that happen:

I. **Work meetings.** Some people just love to meet. Often. Regularly. Sometimes with absolutely no apparent or rational purpose. Their mouse pointer is forever obsessively hovering over the "Create a new meeting" button in Outlook.

These are not People People. These are paid, professional sadists, or nonsadists with very little to do. Sometimes both.

That said, many meetings are motivated by meaningful reasons, but still cause grumbles and moans from invitees long before they even begin. Why? They're tedious and boring and everyone has something better to be doing, like a tax audit or a prostate examination. But the true People People who have scheduled the meeting and are heading it up will take all of that into full consideration. They know instinctively that the first order of business is to keep the natives happy and interested. People People bring treats, snacks, drinks or candies. They begin on time and end on time *or earlier*. The message they communicate is received and perceived because they use humor, visual aids, questions and interactions to keep attention and focus.

Commentary from teammates has an understood limitation on time and relevance. When someone overstays their welcome, the People Person is able to reel them back in or transition to another comment without offending the person and still respecting the good time of others.

2. **Performance evaluation meetings/annual reviews.** Few, if any, employees have any expectations of these meetings being a good time. They are quite possibly delusional if they do. Even star performer, A-list associates have a nervous tickle in their stomachs. But it can be an adventure, a chance to have some fun. The opportunity to hear spectacular words of praise mingled with advice and counsel for improvement. The problem is that most leaders dread these meetings as well. A good T2 People Person will exude a sense of warmth and care and genuine interest in helping develop or correct an employee.

3. **Conference calls.** The only thing that distinguishes a conference call from an in-person meeting is that, when possible, you could be "attending" the meeting in your underwear with *The Price is Right* muted in the background. Either one-on-one or conferencing others in, few people really enjoy the experience. People People have a smile in their voice, a pleasant and nonmonotonous tone and never forget that actual people are on the other end. They speak clearly and just loudly enough, and avoid too much jargon. The phone is impersonal enough as it is, so People People tend to speak in simple, often fun language to liven up the call.

4. **Waiting and long lines.** The DMV, amusement parks, the bank, the grocery store, restaurants, public restrooms, airport security, immigration/passport control, ticket booths, etc. Organizations led by People People will communicate with these disgruntled, captive audiences in at least two ways: to entertain and to inform.

First, they will attempt to lessen the pain of waiting with video screens, TV, signage or music. The messages will be interesting, entertaining, funny and upbeat. They may have People People employees who keep the crowd entertained or informed. A painfully long line at the Viper, one of Six Flags Magic Mountain's popular roller coasters, was made bearable recently when the teenager on the PA added his own quirky personality and style to his frequent announcements. Every two minutes or so, as exhilarated exiting riders were replaced by new ones squeezing into the small seats, this pimply faced teen would intone, "Welcome to the V-v-v-VI-perrrrrr. Woo-wooooooohh!" Park guests slowly inched their way through the serpentine rails of the line giggling at the consistency and unflagging energy with which the kid proudly delivered his line, "Welcome to the V-v-v-VI-perrrrrrrr. Woo-wooooooohh!" It wasn't long before the dull expressions of impatient guests turned to amused grins. Quietly at first, and almost in a mocking tone, a few began chiming in as the boy blared through the cheap speakers. Faces lit up as strangers gave knowing smiles to each other and a feeling of community blossomed. Two minutes later the group sounded like a choir backing a lead singer: "Welcome to the V-v-v-VI-perrrrrrr. Woo-wooooooh!" they chanted in unison. The kid gave them a smile and a thumbs-up.

It's true the end result of this particular waiting experience already *is* a good time, as you hurl through space at 90 miles per hour with both hands bravely held over your head, laughing, screaming and swearing in fear. (Frequently there is another type of hurling associated with these high-speed thrill rides, but it's nobody's idea of a good time.) Still, as Tom Petty once whined, "The waiting is the hardest part." A little slice of unexpected good customer service, the kind that puts a smile on people's faces even during the most boring of waits, is what a People People organization will seek out.

Even a handful of public offices get it. In recent years some DMVs, in an effort to reduce misunderstandings and wait times, have assigned People People to engage customers waiting in line to prescreen them, determine their question or needs, distribute paperwork or point them to another, sometimes faster line. They understand that literally *no one* expects to have a good time at the DMV, but a People Person will try to facilitate a shorter wait and a better experience anyway. This in addition to recruiting and hiring practices that continually strive for more customer service-oriented staff, as opposed to the clichéd "how else may you bother me?" scowling public servant a la Marge Simpson's rude, chain-smoking sisters.

Consider In-N-Out Burger. To enhance communication and customer service while speeding up wait times, often the family-oriented burger chain will send their chipper order takers out in person to the long line of cars waiting in the drive-through lane. What message does this communicate to customers? "We know you're worried about the long line and we understand. Our chefs can only work so fast, and to get your order in before you can even get to the order screen, we'll come help move things along for you." Does this qualify as a good time? For many, yes.

Smart People People companies also use communication strategically to soften wait times—educating the audience on their products or services, sharing messages that build PR and the company reputation. It is done in an entertaining way, thus distracting from the tedium of the waiting and unexpectedly allowing for a good time. Keeping an airport gate full of impatient travelers apprised of the situation is a real People People bit of communication. It serves to quiet the inevitable complaints of "What's going on? Why don't they just tell us what's going on?" It also communicates pertinent information for those wondering about making flight connections at the next airport. On a flight recently the pilot came on the PA and wasted no time, nor beat around the bush: "Folks, from the flight deck, we're sorry about the delay. We've been informed that Air Force One is en route and will be landing shortly. So they've moved us to another runway on the other side. In fact they're moving everyone over there. We're gonna be on the ground for a while." Enhancing the communication with a bit of humor can also ease the tension and provide perspective: "By the way, once we get over to the other runway I imagine we'll be about five hundredth in line for takeoff, so don't jump for joy when you feel us moving." It was a bittersweet laugh, but we all laughed nonetheless and our frustration was tempered.

5. **Job interviews.** What better opportunity can a manager have to establish a working relationship than participating in the interview process with a job candidate? A People Person manager will not only shoot for a great first impression, but will try her best to communicate an accurate depiction of the work culture. She will strive to foster a comfortable, relaxed environment for the interviewee. She will want to learn who this applicant really is, and establishing the right mood is critical for the applicant to want to just be himself. For the jobseeker these interviews are nerve-racking and stressful. They know the job market is tight and candidates are abundant. They arrive in their best clothes and rehearse anticipated answers in the car and elevator. They obsess about bringing up salary requirements or being too excited, pushy or indifferent. In short, each party hopes to have a good time. This will happen if both are committed to relaxing and being themselves, forgetting the pressure they both find themselves under and just communicating. Laughing, smiling, enjoying those few moments of meeting someone new and genuinely striving to connect. Those rare and memorable interviews where both parties walk away excited.

6. **Sales calls/visits.** For being the traditional benchmark of what a People Person is, far too many sales reps these days have lost touch with the soft side. The best salespeople, in

any generation, have always established relationships with clients first. They become a trusted partner in their clients' success. They consultatively sell. But lately, with narrowing profit margins and lower commissions, it seems many sales professionals are less likely to take the time needed to nurture real relationships. They dive right in to close the deal. Quotas are demanding and goals must be met. Yesterday. Many have adopted a proper needs-assessment approach over simply rolling out the menu of services and prices, but by accelerating the process to make the sale sooner have still lost touch with their intuitive people skills. They are serious, demanding, desperate and pushy. The best sales reps patiently stay true to their people values and unleash their personality, wit, humor and soft side in phone calls, texts, e-mails and visits, trusting in their People People instincts. The reality is that person-job fit may need reexamining for some People People sales professionals. Some may find that their long-term relationship strengths don't stack up in a commodities selling environment where clients merely shop price and loyalty means little. A change of scenery and product better suited to a People Person rep might be necessary.

7. **Leadership training.** From your pool of 224 supervisors, managers, directors and others eligible for the training sessions, exactly four are actually quite excited to do it. The rest would prefer to have their gums scraped with a utility knife than spend the day in your learning session. People People know this and work to improve the delivery of the training. Similar to a keynote or other public presentation, an awareness of attendees' low expectations and boredom is paramount. People People make deliberate efforts to keep training sessions as brief as possible while still

communicating the needed materials in a way that will be received, comprehended and retained.

8. School. Absolutely no one enjoys classwork, lectures and tests. Most love the social interactions on a regular basis and the activities and recreational opportunities at recess or in the lunchroom, but no one expects classroom instruction to be a pleasure cruise. Even many of the instructors themselves seem to have about as much excitement for their work as convenience store clerks. What's more, nobody *expects* to enjoy the classroom. Yet legion are the examples of educators who embody People People principles in their classrooms. Rebecca Mieliwocki, a seventh-grade English teacher in Burbank, California, was honored at the White House by being named 2012 National Teacher of the Year.

According to Los Angeles's *Daily Breeze*:

> Mieliwocki is known for unconventional techniques developed during her 13-year teaching career, the last nine spent at Burbank Middle School.
>
> She inscribes playing cards with students' names, with the luck of the draw determining who gets called on to read in class. A ding from a hotel service bell on her desk signals a correct answer.
>
> Mieliwocki also understands the fast pace of information bombarding today's adolescents and has set up her lesson plan to capture and retain their attention. She might play music on her iPod while students work on a classroom assignment or inject a story about growing up in Napa, where her parents were both teachers.[2]

Mieliwocki said on CBS *This Morning* that she believes her "number one job . . . is to educate [her students] and to give them the skills they need to be successful" in any career. She tries to do that by being "creative [and] lively." She said she's "happy to be there every day" and admitted she enjoys teaching middle schoolers partly because "deep down inside I'm 12 years old."[3]

There's certainly a fine line between entertaining the troops, giving them latitude, allowing some frivolity and maintaining control, respect for authority and credibility. People People work hard to find the right mix and don't just give up in the face of pressure.

9. **Church.** Where is it written that an hour or two of worship each week must be devoid of laughter, humor and joy? Clergy of all faiths are waking up to the needs of their constituents in a sermon setting. While some traditional faiths employ the services of a single leader to preach the good word, other faiths understand the importance of variety and improvisation. Asking different people from the congregation to prepare messages and talks each week is a smart way to keep people's attention. They are encouraged to use personal stories and examples with scriptures to mix in some variety. Religious services need not be completely devoid of appropriate doses of humor as long as the intent is to inspire and compel. But the point of a church meeting, as I see it, is to extricate ourselves from the mundane and take a break from the daily grind of the world. Focusing our energy and devotion to God once a week shouldn't be too much of a stretch for most People People. So while it's a much-welcomed change to mix in a little levity or share non-Bible stories in a church talk, the focus should be clear and the mood appropriate. The use of proper music, choirs and other performances should

reinforce the purpose of the message, not distract from or upstage it.

10. **Funerals.** Can a good time *be* had at a funeral or wake? Most contemporary funeral directors or clergy are exceptional People People and have learned to perfectly blend levity, warmth, compassion and perspective. Too often, however, family members, friends and other eulogists are reluctant to celebrate the life of the deceased, thus ensuring that grieving continues for both family mourners and innocent audience members. This even occurs at funerals where the death was no big surprise to anyone, and even hoped for due to extended physical suffering. Grieving is appropriate and healthy, of course, and the funeral done with proper respect allows survivors to reach some degree of closure. But telling funny stories, using humor and laughter in eulogies and speeches, is welcomed and needed. People People know when the time is right for laughter or tears. They can hug and hold someone, offering a shoulder to cry on, as easily as they can flash a smile to cheer someone up. The same of course could be said when it comes to the next item on this list . . .

11. **Hospital visits and stays.** Patients have enough gravitas to deal with without you dropping by to add your two cents of sad face. People People may not don a Patch Adams clown nose or make a bouquet of fake flowers magically appear out of the thin air of their jacket sleeve, but they will laugh and be lively. They are, after all, stopping by to *cheer up* the patient. As with funerals, however, the tragedy or seriousness of each instance must be considered.

Engaging Communications

What makes a newsman like *NBC Nightly News*'s Brian Williams a People Person? It takes a little more investigation than merely switching over to NBC to watch him read the news. Sure, there's a certain amount of humanity in his delivery and the occasional bit of tongue in cheekiness. He's pleasant and straightforward, with a sincerity that boosts credibility. But if you've spent more than a few hours a week watching television in the last few years you'll have seen Mr. Williams making guest appearances on other NBC programs such as *30 Rock, Saturday Night Live, The Today Show* and on other networks in a decidedly non-news-anchor way. In short, Brian Williams has a sense of humor and play. He may take his job seriously, but he doesn't let it define who he is.

Williams understands that he is a brand. He represents the authority and authenticity of all that is NBC News. And yet there he is, late Saturday night, dressed as a construction worker with a thick New York accent playing a character that evokes belly laughs from a stingy audience. Why do they laugh so hard? The incongruity of a straightlaced, buttoned-down news anchor playing the fool on live TV . . . and he's not bad!

Where credibility is king in the high-stakes game of television news ratings, Williams and indeed NBC run a costly risk. Viewers demand their anchors be serious, straightforward and somber, don't they? Otherwise it would be difficult to take them at their word, or trust them to be objective and complete in their reports. Right? It was certainly true in the days of Edward R. Murrow and Walter Cronkite, when news reporters sucked on cigarettes and stared gravely at the viewing audience while delivering the grim news of the world they lived in. This grave tone indicated a kind of authority and credibility to their reports.

But times, they have a-changed.

We are a global society of consumers with short attention spans. We demand a rapid and almost constant flow of information to keep us interested. Tell me about the earthquake in Moldova and you might capture my attention. Show me footage and I'm rapt. We also seek sources that entertain us while they enlighten us. *The Daily Show,* Stephen Colbert and Glenn Beck are examples of information sources that mix fact, half truths, rumors and stories with humor and parody. A People Person is someone who understands this about her fellow humans. She will do her level best to keep her listener, viewer or audience attentive and engaged. *NBC Nightly News,* with its debatably humorous, media-loving lead anchor Williams, is consistently and perhaps not surprisingly number one in the ratings. For several years running they have kept the top position in the highly competitive numbers race.

There's no business like show business. Undoubtedly the grating femme baritone of Ethel Merman is echoing in your head right now. Annoying little show tune that won't go away. But ask yourself this laughably obvious question: If there's no business like show business, then why shouldn't your business be a little more showy? Or at least your communications.

For example, anyone can pick up a book and read it. Books evoke imagery, enlighten minds and motivate action. But that's a personal experience unfolding in someone's head and heart. The same could be said for written reports and proposals. So why would anyone asked to present a report, proposal or paper merely stand up, open her mouth and read aloud? Save everyone time and send it in an e-mail. They can read it themselves. Otherwise, connect with them. Add value to the time your audience is taking away from their hot-button projects, phone calls and tasks that are forever in need of attention, especially if they could simply read your message.

A professional colleague and good friend of mine, Chester Elton, has made a very comfortable living as a best-selling author. He and coauthor Adrian Gostick have sold over a million copies of their business books— *The Carrot Principle, All In,* and *The Orange Revolution,* to name a few. But ask Chester what's made him a millionaire and he'll tell you it's traveling the globe speaking about those books. People are willing to part with, technically speaking, gobs of money to secure Chester for their conferences and meetings. He's that good. And here's why. What Chester does can't be replicated. He's not a typical author/speaker. Chester's a People Person, so he delivers more than just compelling content. He's hilarious, engaging, witty and smart. He's loud and brash, calm and sincere. His PowerPoint slides are entertaining, bright, well timed and laugh-out-loud funny. Sure, devotees could just read his books, but Chester brings them to *life*. His is a gift that few author/speakers—even those who are far more well known and who've sold millions more books—simply don't have.

You have to have a *hook*. To keep them listening and engaged is going to boil down to four possible scenarios:

> **Scenario 1:** You have *killer* material. Your subject matter is of such import, interest and immediate applicability to your audience that they are literally poised pen in hand, edge of seat, ears perked up awaiting your every syllable, even though you are about as watchable as a bucket of smelt. The hook? Content. And to be fair, the only content that can stand on its own in engaging an audience, regardless of who delivers it and how, will be prurient, sensational, violent or a meeting to discuss bonuses. A lawn chair could deliver the presentation and would get a standing ovation.

> **Scenario 2:** Your topic is about as riveting as a cricket match. Why on earth anyone called this meeting or chose this subject is a total mystery. It is likely some kind of compulsory class or presentation for certification purposes. Nevertheless, you have a captive audience. The hook? *You.*

Scenario 3: You are a charismatic and likable presenter and your subject is quite important. But it's nothing new, neither groundbreaking nor earth shattering, so you're planning to deliver the material in a way that compels them to perk up, take notes and engage. The hook? Still you.

Scenario 4: The topic is terrible and you're terrible. The hook? The donuts and coffee promised to all attendees or the free lunch afterward.

Any way you shake it, make no mistake: there must be a hook. Something to keep them there and listening (or pretending to, at least). You *owe* the audience. At conferences or seminars, more often than not there is a fee to attend. Your audience has literally paid to hear your presentation. You must deliver more than just walking them through your bullet points. And that includes those free meetings held for your own employees in the J. Edgar Hoover Memorial Training Room and Cafeteria Annex. Even though they get paid to be there, you still owe them. There are lost opportunities, time, resources, sometimes travel and other costs associated with these internal meetings. Never forget, you are in their debt. A People Person needs little reminding of this in communicating messages.

The key to successfully winning the hearts of an audience is being genuine, just being yourself. Humor is a fine line, and for some, even the most confident of People People, a risky proposition. Self-deprecating is a good way to go; it's an easy way to ingratiate yourself to an audience. It puts them on your side and appeals to their sense of compassion. It's not uncommon to hear a group "awwwwww" in response to a speaker kicking his own butt. "I think most of you here know what a lousy golfer I am. No, no, it's true. I spend so much time hacking away at the weeds the groundskeeper offered me a part-time job."

Using Humor in Public Speech

Here are a few basic concepts regarding humor in public communications:

1. **Make sure it's appropriate to the audience and occasion.** A safe, simple rule is to plan humor that only relates to the topic, theme or attendees. Straying outside these lines puts you at risk for failure.

2. **Keep it real.** Only use traditional jokes and punch lines if you've tried them out on a practice audience first. And make sure they relate. Keeping your mood light is usually more entertaining than planned shtick anyway. If you're smiling and have a bit of an unplanned, spontaneous feel to your delivery, you're more likely to stumble onto something humorous that you can develop as you continue.

3. **Interact with the audience.** With few exceptions, the funniest stuff happens when you don't plan it. You'll put yourself in a position for some crowd-pleasing levity when you engage in conversation with an attendee.

Using PowerPoint (or Whatever)

My professional secrets of a world-class, kick-butt presentation are the stuff of memoirs. I will write a book of tips someday when I'm off the market and no longer competing for business with the other 37 billion public speakers. I will probably be seventy-seven at the time that I finally retire, and by then all keynote speeches will be beamed to your mind from a guy sitting in his—what else?—underwear in his home office.

Until then, one secret I will share is to use PowerPoint, or Keynote or whatever presentation software you like. Many gurus can get away with being the sole focus of a presentation. They don't need visuals. These people are just so smart, engaging, important, famous, authoritative, charismatic, good looking, funny or just flat-out awesome that they themselves, alone, can hold the riveted attention of an audience for thirty, sixty, seventy-five minutes.

The rest of us here on earth need a little help. In fact, if I were to share my deepest, personal feelings on the matter, I might say that after a couple of minutes even an all-powerful guru just standing there talking could stand a little infusion of energy that supporting media can provide. Studies among university business class professors and their students regarding the effectiveness of using PowerPoint in lectures have drawn few surprising conclusions: teachers tend to overvalue the impact of PowerPoint in cognitive learning, but class attendance is higher when it is used regularly in lectures, and students and teachers both believe that PowerPoint promotes enhanced note taking, content recall during exams, emphasis of key points and attention holding.[4]

In the world of business presentations or keynote speeches, the emphasis is less on learning transfer and more on creating an emotional impact. You want your audience to be motivated, excited, laughing, crying, rapt or whatever. Using visuals and other tools that support your point enhances the possibilities. The risk of PowerPoint is buying into the fallacy that it will turn a bad presentation into a good one or convert an ineffective presentation into an effective one. The truth is it can make a good presentation even better, if used wisely. PowerPoint shouldn't replace you as the main focus, but I believe that too many people shy away from using it to maximum effect as much as they could. A People Person will happily apply whatever instrument will aid in conveying the message well, and also acknowledges the speaker's debt to the audience.

Communication for Generation Text

Years ago People People would say that nothing was as impersonal as a telephone conversation, that the best conversations happen face to face. The invention of the telephone not surprisingly coincided with an upswing in the average human's weight and attendant health risks like heart disease and diabetes. In 1900, the average weight of a twenty-year-old male was 133 pounds. Today it's 166. For women, 122 and 144. Men are only slightly taller, not enough to justify another 33 pounds. Women have remained about the same height.[5]

The telephone made life easier to be sure, but speeding up communications was not without a cost, as it slowed down people skills. The art of letter writing has waned to the point of near extinction today. We also sacrificed our personal, live interaction with all its subtle visual cues, body language and eye contact at the altar of invention.

"It is my heart-warm and world-embracing Christmas hope and aspiration that all of us, the high, the low, the rich, the poor, the admired, the despised, the loved, the hated, the civilized, the savage (every man and brother of us all throughout the whole earth), may eventually be gathered together in a heaven of everlasting rest and peace and bliss, except the inventor of the telephone." A version of this quote by Mark Twain first appeared in the *Boston Daily Globe* in 1890.[6]

In today's e-universe the tables have turned. Where the telephone once seemed merely a fancy contraption that made messenger services, perfumed letters written in cursive and actual visits to a friend or family member obsolete, a telephone call is now considered by many the rarest form of human communication, an effort of personal touch too strenuous to regularly consider. Heaven forbid someone should attempt to communicate beyond texting or typing the message. Why, you might as well be seated on the veranda sipping lemonade and whispering words of woo to your lady friend than be so personal as to talk on the telephone to another human.

And to think it hasn't been much more than a couple of decades since parents nagged their children to "get off the phone already!" because it was a sinful waste of time to lounge about twirling the phone cord into knots during an hours-long conversation about who wore what to the roller rink. Today those former phone-call-obsessed teens of an earlier era would give up their iPads and Netflix membership (temporarily) to see any of their children actually talking to someone on a telephone. Many nostalgics even enjoy the kitschy cell phone ringtones that sound like the old rotary telephones that hung on the kitchen wall. How forlorn and lonely the few remaining telephone booths appear in airports, hospitals and 7-Elevens. And try finding a phone book to rip in half in a drunken wager of raw strength. But that's another story.

Setting aside the pointless yearning for the past, as well as the present advantages of light-speed technology in computers and handheld devices, is the art of telephone conversations forever lost, and if so, is mourning merited? Do the younger generations, or even the well-adapted older tech users, really need to brush up on their phone skills? People People adamantly say "yes." They never stop seeking opportunities to connect with other people in "live" mode. Cutting-edge technology be hanged. And it's not just the traditional belief that People People prefer the personal touch of a human voice, though many certainly do. They simply understand that real-time, spoken messages are more effective and efficient communications. They care. They want the message to be clear and understood without wasting anyone's time. E-mails and text messages can be misconstrued, like this exchange between Dave and Lisa:

Hey Dave,
Just wondering if you wanted to spend a few minutes going over your presentation with me before you jump in front of the board.
Lisa
* * *

Lisa,

Thanks, but not sure that's necessary. I mean it's totally done and I wouldn't be able to incorporate any changes at this point. Besides, Jim's already bought off on it, so maybe I'm not sure what you're asking.

Dave

* * *

Dave,

I just thought you might like to practice with someone.

Lisa

* * *

Lisa,

What makes you think I need to practice it so much? What have you heard about it?

Dave

* * *

Dave,

I haven't heard a thing. Is there something wrong with it?

Lisa

* * *

Lisa,

No, nothing's wrong with it. Jim has already approved it.

Dave

* * *

Dave,

Okay, just forget it then. Good luck.

Lisa

* * *

Lisa,

Fine. If you really want to help, maybe you could just spend a few minutes with me as I go over the presentation. It might be nice to have someone to just listen to it before I get in front of the board.

Dave

This conversation could have taken thirty seconds on the phone or face-to-face, and without the misunderstanding, paranoia and hurt feelings.

> LISA: *"Hey Dave, if you want I could sit in while you practice your presentation."*
> DAVE: *"It's pretty late in the game and I can't make any more changes."*
> LISA: *"No, I just meant I could be an audience member for you, if that would help you out at all."*
> DAVE: *"Oh. Perfect. Yes, thanks."*

Electronic messages may not accurately convey a person's intent, mood, sincerity or humor. So where space and time constraints prevent an in-person visit, People People will prefer a phone call over an e-mail or a text. Research shows that they're not entirely alone. A recent survey of nearly 2,300 U.S. adults found that while 73 percent of them use text messaging, 51 percent would prefer a phone call compared to 31 percent who would prefer receiving a text; 14 percent said it depends on the situation. As of September 2011, most adults still made more cell phone calls than sent or received texts each day, but that gap has almost closed.[7]

People People, of course, have the ability to do both—talk or text—and know the most appropriate times to use those skills. But too many people are losing their ability to have the traditional face-to-face conversations that are vital in the workplace and personal relationships.

A 2011 survey reported that 45 percent of American teenagers send at least thirty text messages a day.[8] That number seems laughably low by today's standards, doesn't it? My thirteen-year-old sends thirty texts—to five different people—while working on his first math problem for homework! "It is an art that's becoming as valuable as good writing," said Janet Sternberg, a professor of communication and media studies at Fordham University in New York.[9]

Sternberg has noticed that more and more students have trouble with the most basic aspects of direct conversation, including the inability to look her in the eye when talking to her. Those are things that will not serve them very well as they enter a world where many will still expect them to be able to carry on a face-to-face conversation, or at the very least manage the occasional phone call.

Many professors say they rarely see students outside of class. "I sit in my office hours lonely now because if students have a question, they email, often late at night," said Renee Houston, associate professor of communication studies at the University of Puget Sound in Washington State. "And they never call, ever."[10]

Interpersonal skills are more important in the workplace than IT skills, according to the results of a survey commissioned by Microsoft. In the survey of approximately five hundred board-level executives, 61 percent said interpersonal and teamworking skills were more important than IT skills.[11]

However, according to Microsoft chairman Bill Gates, while communication skills are important, "one of the most important changes of the past 30 years is that digital technology has transformed almost everyone into an information worker."[12] In almost every job now, people use software and work with information to enable their organization to operate more effectively."

But Gates acknowledged that "communication skills and the ability to work well with different types of people are very important too. Software innovation, like almost every other kind of innovation, requires the ability to collaborate and share ideas with other people, and to sit down and talk with customers and get their feedback and understand their needs."[13]

Mr. Gates's perfectly stated explanation of Type III communication skills—the ability to collaborate, sit down and talk *and* understand other people's needs—is a good way to close this chapter. It's that rare but obtainable combination of T1 people *skills* with a T2 *concern* for people.

CHAPTER EIGHT

Enjoy life; there's plenty of time to be dead. —*Hans Christian Andersen*

A May 2012 study by the Rheingold Institute reported that more and more Germans are incapable of enjoying life. The Cologne-based research group found that 46 percent of Germans say they are increasingly unable to enjoy anything due to the stress of everyday life. Among the study's younger participants, 55 percent claim to have lost their ability to feel good. One of the researchers commented, "Our joy gene is increasingly defective—we've forgotten how to enjoy ourselves."[1] Germans deliberately work very hard so they can enjoy rare moments of leisure; they need to feel that they've earned those moments. But when they finally get to their well-deserved timeout, they feel guilt and pressure and can't relax.

Undoubtedly, a tough European economy and Germany's role in bailing out the rest of the continent are major factors in their collective sense of "no time for timeouts." But Germans have long had a reputation for being serious, dispassionate and joyless. So what else is new?

People People can be found in any nation, on every continent. Even Deutschland. How else do you explain Oktoberfest and German chocolate cake? People of all nationalities, races and genders are either born with or can develop a little thing I like to call *perspective*. (Others call it perspective, too. I mean, I don't own it.)

Just Happy to Be Here

In Chapter Seven I mentioned two different kinds of gratitude. In that chapter we learned about the *act* of gratitude: thanking others, expressing appreciation, recognizing efforts. People People also deliberately foster a *feeling* of gratitude, a sense of appreciation for who they are, what they have and the day-to-day adventure of life. It's that perspective that shapes their decisions, informs their moods and allows them to smile and laugh more. Keeping things in perspective is a highly sought-after quality that aspiring People People must obtain. Once obtained, they will use that perspective as the baseline for their decisions, actions and reactions.

I mentioned earlier that I'm a soccer fan. When I'm on the road, I often relax by watching a match on TV; doesn't matter who's playing whom. It could be the Madagascar Girl's Under-13 Tournament and I'd be fine. One international match I saw featured the Nigerian men's national team against a very powerful team from another country. I can't remember the opponent, but they were the clear favorites over Nigeria. It was a semifinal, all-or-nothing, win-or-go-home match—a lot on the line. The Nigerian crowd was excited and energetic, engaged in every play, loudly cheering on their heroes. They sang and danced together and enjoyed the atmosphere. The frequent television shots of the Nigerian faithful captured their bright smiles and high spirits.

Their team fought hard, and late into the second half were still tied at zero. With less than ten minutes remaining, however, the other team finally scored a goal. The Nigerian fans, despite falling behind and facing the reality that they would probably be eliminated from the tournament, continued to smile and dance and enjoy themselves. There wasn't a collective shriek of despair from the Nigerian stands. There were no violent shouts at the officials or bemoaning every suspicious no-call. There were no looks of shock or panic. No one was contemplating suicide. The fans simply kept on cheering and smiling and supporting their team. They were clearly proud of how far the team had come, far surpassing expectations. They had felt surges of excitement, pride and fun. They were grateful to have gotten that far and to have seen a good match. But now it was over. Okay. Time to go. No harm done. They had been entertained. (Some British fans, on the other hand, would have ripped their seats out, constructed a barricade, thrown roadside flares at their own players and kidnapped a referee.)

Perspective makes enjoyment possible.

I learned to appreciate live sporting events from a similar perspective when I worked in radio. Being an absolute sports nut, I took full advantage of my "press" status to secure credentials to every Utah Jazz and BYU football home game for several seasons. Cozily ensconced courtside or up in a comfy, catered press suite, I soon realized that membership came with a cost: absolutely no cheering. As a "reporter," it is not professional to root for any team; you must be a neutral observer. You are simply there to cover the action, get some postgame quotes in the locker rooms and report the news. Did I mention the free banquet spread before each game and snacks at halftime? Tough duty. Anyway, exorcising the instinct to leap out of my seat or high five the guy next to me when our home team made an amazing play took some getting used to. Often two or three of us "homers" would wince or flinch in synch, restraining our twitch muscles from acting out their natural responses as we quickly looked to see if anyone noticed our inappropriate excitement.

Eventually I got to the point where I could simply watch a game without emoting. Particularly when the home team wasn't winning, it got easier to just enjoy the spectacle of the game itself and the entertainment the action provided. To this day, I still don't jump and cheer and scream and yell like I used to. It allows me to not be too emotionally invested in the outcome. Win or lose, I just appreciate a good game. The spectacle, the bright colors, the jaw-dropping athleticism. It all makes me happy, regardless of the game's result.

Kurt Vonnegut, in his book *A Man Without a Country* (2005), suggests that the real problem is not that we are rarely happy but that we don't realize when we are happy, and that we should get in the habit of noticing those moments and stop and savor them. He wrote:

I apologize to all of you who are the same age as my grandchildren. And many of you reading this are probably the same age as my grandchildren. They, like you, are being royally shafted and lied to by our Baby Boomer corporations and government.

Yes, this planet is in a terrible mess. But it has always been a mess. There have never been any "Good Old Days," there have just been days. And as I say to my grandchildren, "Don't look at me, I just got here."

There are old poops who will say that you do not become a grown-up until you have somehow survived, as they have, some famous calamity—the Great Depression, the Second World War, Vietnam, whatever. Storytellers are responsible for this destructive, not to say suicidal, myth. Again and again in stories, after some terrible mess, the character is able to say at last, "Today I am a woman. Today I am a man. The end."

When I got home from the Second World War, my Uncle Dan clapped me on the back, and he said, "You're a man now." So I killed him. Not really, but I certainly felt like doing it.

Dan, that was my bad uncle, who said a man can't be a man unless he'd gone to war.

But I had a good uncle, my late Uncle Alex. He was my father's kid brother, a childless graduate of Harvard who was an honest life-insurance salesman in Indianapolis. He was well-read and wise. And his principal complaint about other human beings was that they so seldom noticed it when they were happy. So when we were drinking lemonade under an

CHAPTER NINE

apple tree in the summer, say, and talking lazily about this and that, almost buzzing like honeybees, Uncle Alex would suddenly interrupt the agreeable blather to exclaim, "If this isn't nice, I don't know what is."

So I do the same now, and so do my kids and grandkids. And I urge you to please notice when you are happy, and exclaim or murmur or think at some point, "If this isn't nice, I don't know what is."[2]

It's sage advice from someone who's lived a little. Recognize happy times and be grateful for them. Sure, but what about the tough times? People People more often than not *choose* happiness. For them it is unconditional, independent of how well things are going or how much lemonade is flowing under a shady tree on a lazy summer afternoon. Martin Luther King put it this way: "The ultimate measure of a man is not where he stands in moments of comfort and convenience, but where he stands at times of challenge and controversy."[3]

Joy in the Journey

Tiger Woods is accustomed to winning. And when he does, his big toothy grin is difficult to miss. But most of the time Tiger is a Jerk. That's not just my totally biased opinion, it's a fact. He's a moping, groaning, cursing baby. He slams his clubs down and broods. Practically every other golfer out there is smiling, happy, shrugging their shoulders, waving to the crowd . . . enjoying the ride. Woods only breaks into a grin and a fist pump when he holes a seemingly impossible shot out of a steep-faced sand trap or when some other stroke goes his way. The TV announcers continue to sell his immaturity as "intense focus," but most of the audience doesn't buy it. They know what they see: a guy who demands perfection from himself and rarely looks up to enjoy the blessings of a beautiful day on a breathtaking landscape in front of thousands of adoring fans, and the opportunity to make more money by finishing in forty-seventh place then most of them will take home in a year.

One of the men long considered Woods's closest rival is Phil Mickelson, himself a proven winner on the links, and the kind of guy you'd trust with your wallet, car keys and youngest daughter. He smiles. He laughs. He's nice to the gallery. Win or lose. Has Mickelson suffered his share of meltdowns and defeats? Of course; especially off the golf course, things that *really* matter. He took most of 2009 off to be home with the family and to support his wife while she dealt with breast cancer. Not long after, he was inflicted with arthritis. He manages to keep up good spirits and take things in stride. Phil Mickelson has that perspective that enables him to enjoy the ride.

Do People People get sad? Feel pain and discomfort? Yearn for more? Do they suffer from doubt, uncertainty and fears? Do they choke? Lose their tempers? Act like a Jerk? Yes. But they maintain a constant undercurrent of optimism and perspective that is often outwardly manifested by their words, actions, laughs and smiles. "Laughing through the tears" is more than a quaint expression; it is the bedrock attitude of happy people.

Finding joy in the journey is one of life's greatest tests. For years I lived next door to a man who had suffered physical injuries, surgeries, family crises and underemployment. The barrage of affliction seemed to be continual, simultaneous and, naturally, undeserved. But this man would arise early each morning, whistling, to face another day of work. His cheery, random whistling—you know the kind: no specific tune, just spontaneous composition of something that sounds musical—could be heard through my bedroom window. It was a daily reminder that we choose happiness. The neighbor always greeted me with a smile, a handshake and an upbeat attitude. It would have been easy to launch into a lengthy "woe is me" pity patter, but he deliberately kept his problems to himself. He didn't want to bring others down with his sad affairs.

In fact, consider the ten happiest jobs from 2011, according to the National Organization for Research at the University of Chicago.[4] It's not a stretch to see the link to People People:

CHAPTER NINE

1. **Clergy.** Imagine. Those who give up the world to serve others full-time are the happiest of all. Not all of them are persuasive communicators or social butterflies, but their life's work is about loving and caring for people.

2. **Firefighters.** This job is *all* about helping and serving others. Can you imagine someone eulogizing one of these heroes and telling the grieving family, "Though not what I'd call a 'people person,' John was a great guy nonetheless"?

3. **Physical therapists.** Again, helping others brings great joy and a high degree of job satisfaction. The best PTs have genuine concern for their clients. Being engaging and personable is a definite advantage, but not an absolute requirement.

4. **Authors.** No people skills required, but no money made either (unless you're J. K. Rowling or Stephen King). They're happy because they enjoy autonomy and a vehicle to express themselves. What's more, and good news for novel readers, some brain-mapping research has concluded that "individuals who frequently read fiction seem to be better able to understand other people, empathize with them and see the world from their perspective."[5] In other words, *Harry Potter and the Prisoner of Azkaban* may not exactly be a Pulitzer Prize winner, but it can help your people skills.

5. **Special education teachers.** Low salaries; high satisfaction. They may not be the life of any party or strike up wonderful conversations with total strangers in line at Piggly Wiggly, but these compassionate, patient educators are People People through and through.

6. Teachers. Scandalously underpaid, but happy. Is that possible? Yes. Why? Most are People People. Most. Some are decidedly not.

7. Artists. Fulfilling their need to create, many want to ennoble mankind and provide beauty for others to enjoy. When it happens, they're happy.

8. Psychologists. This is a bit surprising and flies in the face of common belief. Many people think that psychologists are a sad lot, having reputedly entered the field to find a cure for their own problems. Evidently enough of them have forgotten about themselves and find happiness in helping others.

9. Financial services sales agents. Okay, this one is mostly about the money. But being good at it requires a level of humanity that anyone can have, beyond just T1 persuasive salesmanship.

10. Operating engineers. We're talking about bulldozers, backhoes and big-boy, real-world Tonka trucks. How unhappy could you be?

Below is my own less-than-scientifically-proven list of the happiest jobs for People People:

1. Whatever job they currently have.

Overall, People People are happier than Everyone Else. If being a People Person merely meant having a bubbly personality or a yen for group inclusion (T1), you could poke holes in the notion. But because fully (or partially) developed People People strive for "people first," their happiness is deep and lasting. They are sincere in their concern for others. It is not a temporary or passing interest based solely on their own short- or long-term wants, needs or desires. Their happiness does not depend on positive outcomes only. If People People don't get their way it may sting briefly, but it does not permanently alter their relationships with or attitudes toward their peers, bosses, family or close friends.

Studies have shown a strong relationship between happiness and outward-focused activities. One rather obvious report found that happy people enjoy playing sports, playing and reading with children, socializing with family and friends, having meals at home and making sweet, sweet love more than solo activities like yard work, paying bills, grocery shopping, car repair and doctor visits. Well, duh! The former activities are fun, amusing, enriching, pleasurable and satisfying emotionally, physically, even spiritually. The reason sad people are sad is because they're *not* doing those things. This same study found that people who spend the most time watching television are the least happy in the long run. Happy people still watch and enjoy TV, but not to excess. They know it is generally a waste of time, but sometimes an enjoyable one. A major predictor of how much time is spent watching television is whether someone works or not. When unemployment is high, it is likely that people (unhappy, unemployed people) will watch more television.[6]

The antidote? Turn outward and engage in activities that include or benefit others. People People look for opportunities to put others first in any activity. They include their spouses or children in yard work, teaching them how to weed or to mow the lawn. They invite a child to come with them to the grocery store. They talk in the car and have them "run missions" in the store. They may pause and chat with a neighbor in the aisle, asking how things are. Paying bills may be an undesirable must-do chore, but People People can use the time to teach kids about how to write a check or use a balance book.

A Sense of Humor

In a previous book on levity, my coauthor and I acknowledged the importance of developing your own sense of humor, play and fun. For example, one study found those with a sense of humor climbed the corporate ladder faster and made more money than their peers. We published important research on the connection between lightening up at work and employee retention, satisfaction and engagement. In terms of employee retention alone, the 90 percent of workers who rated their boss's sense of humor highest had zero intention of bugging out.[7]

A sense of humor is an absolute must for People People, but understand this: *Having a sense of humor doesn't necessarily mean that you have to be funny.* Certainly you have plenty of friends or acquaintances that you would say have a good sense of humor, but not all of them tell jokes or make you laugh. You don't have to be the humor *giver*; more often than not you will simply be the humor *receiver*. Or at the very least a humor appreciator/allower/tolerator.

More often than not, humor is less about being funny than it is about being fun. There are a handful of comedy geniuses among us whose minds are continually generating comebacks, one-liners, plays on words, puns and the like, but the majority of us are just content to contribute an amusing reactive phrase or share a funny personal story. We enjoy some frivolity. For as serious as our jobs may be, fun and play are critical to enjoying the daily grind.

A survey of 38,000 people, mostly millennials or Gen Y'ers, found that 94 percent say at least some fun at work is okay, with the majority of all respondents (63 percent) saying that they like a good balance of levity and seriousness.[8]

Even the Great Place to Work Institute concurs that having fun at work is critical in building a trusting work environment. Amy Lyman, cofounder of the institute, shared data in *The Levity Effect* that concluded that companies that didn't make the "great" list had significantly lower

CHAPTER NINE

fun scores. "Any company that wants to be 'great,' should be wondering how to have more fun," Lyman told us.[9] A 2011 peek at their research found that "this is a fun place to work" is the second most highly correlated statement to the overall "great place to work" statement, trailing only "I'm proud to tell others I work here" by a few thousandths of a point.

Ahhh, Laughter

Enjoying the ride will inevitably involve ample laughter, but People People are careful to avoid negative, derisive, demeaning or prejudicial levity. Somehow they manage to share lighter moments with associates without having to resort to offensive language or content. I'm not suggesting that all People People are prudes or Sunday Jims, but there is a natural inclination toward keeping things clean.

But laughter just feels good, doesn't it? If you instinctively agree with the adage "laughter does a body good," then you've likely experienced the very real, therapeutic effects of laughing. There's a reason People People live longer than Jerks. For one thing, the Jerkier you are the higher the risk of being wiped off the face of the earth by another Jerk. But the more a People Person keeps a happy outlook, smiles and, especially, laughs, the better off physically they are.

Here are four specific ways laughing it up is great for your physical health:

1. **It relaxes the whole body.** Those big, full-body laughs relieve tension and decrease stress hormones, and leave your muscles relaxed for up to forty-five minutes.

2. **It boosts the immune system.** It increases immune cells and infection-fighting antibodies, improving your resistance to disease.

3. **It triggers the release of endorphins.** These feel-good chemicals promote an overall sense of well-being, and can even temporarily relieve pain.

4. **It protects the heart.** By improving the function of blood vessels and increasing blood flow, laughter can help protect you against a heart attack and other cardiovascular problems.[10]

People People apply the principle of latitude (from Chapter Seven) when it comes to others' enjoyment. Who's to say what's fun or funny and what isn't? Just because you don't think something's funny doesn't mean it isn't funny; it just isn't funny to *you*. There's no be-all and end-all judge who determines what constitutes a "good time" for people. And if it turns out that there is, well, I'd be surprised if it turned out to be me or you. So unless jocularity exceeds legal limits or what is deemed proper in a work environment—as the crowd chanted in *The Bad News Bears in Breaking Training*—"Let them play!"

CHAPTER TEN
"People People" People People and Final Thoughts

Let's face it, human resources people get a bad rap no matter how you slice it. Whether you're the solemn bearer of bad news like the abolishing of Casual Fridays or the cheery messenger of another Weight Watchers group weight loss record, people just don't like you. The sooner you come to grips, the sooner the searing, sharp pains subside. One of the top reasons you are the eternal object of vilification and death threats is because you represent the mean old junior high librarian or the uptight gym teacher or the absolutely intolerant substitute. You're the enforcer, the wet towel, the sourpuss, the buzzkill . . . you get the idea.

Can something be done? Yes. You can quit your job and go to work at your father's accounting firm or pursue your dream to be a fashion designer. Or you can take to heart the concepts in this book and promise yourself that you'll become more *human* than *resource*.

I know I'm making some broad generalizations and it's not fair. Because the truth is that those "great companies" I've referred to, and a million others like them, have *amazing* HR leaders that are the absolute epitome of fully developed Type III People People.

Kaye Jorgensen was the executive vice president of human resources—the headmistress of evil—at a large manufacturing facility for nearly thirty years. When she retired, a company-wide event was held not to celebrate and revel in her departure, but to honor and revere her. People actually cried. Imagine. Shouldn't they have been singing "Ding dong, the witch is dead"? How could this happen, you wonder? Because Jorgensen was down-to-earth, easygoing, fun and smart. She cared about people, not processes. She led, not managed. She poked fun at herself and her profession. She was laid back, casual and accessible. She wisely wielded humor while still performing her sworn duties. (Does HR *have* a sworn oath?)

More Human Than Resources

I recently spoke to a large group of financial advisors and leaders at a multinational's quarterly meeting in Toronto. Before every keynote I give, there's always a telephone call, typically with the VP of HR, to get briefed on particulars. The reason she specifically wanted me to come was to encourage their people to lighten up, and to give them permission to enjoy themselves more at work. I was told this was a group of mostly serious, buttoned-down financial professionals who had lofty goals and pressure to perform. My high-energy, interactive and hilarious (her words, not mine) presentation would immediately follow messages delivered by a couple of executives.

For me, this was the perfect tee-up. I assumed these two suits would bore them to tears, allowing me to close the show with an audience dying to laugh. But the HR VP had insisted that the two executives keep it light, make it fun, lighten up and be real. And they obeyed—much to my horror! In a room of 450 client reps, advisors, managers and administrators, they told jokes, poked fun at themselves and others, showed funny slides and elicited authentic, nonsycophantic laughs. They did this while delivering relevant, pertinent business information and motivation. They engaged their audience and made it memorable.

By the time I went on, I was confident I'd been upstaged. And I had been. So I really turned up the juice. I was all over the room, joking with a guy in the back, purposely mispronouncing names of people up front, throwing Frisbees and tee shirts, cracking one-liners and ad-libs at hyperspeed, even tossing out throwaway jokes about Canada, their bosses and the company name, always keeping one eye on the HR leader who had brought me in. She laughed hardest of all!

That VP of HR, like others in her position, has figured out that she represents the link to encouraging the development of People People within her organization. Who better to sponsor the notion of People People than the *head* of the people department? Every company has People People, to be sure, some more well known than others. And those people spread their influence around in random patterns. It's hit and miss. Some senior- and executive-level People People lead by example and hope that others will emulate their ways. But it's the HR leaders and their staff that are *expected* to embrace and encourage humanity among the workforce.

It's the *people* people that develop People People.

Julie Dongju Lee is the director of human resources at the JW Marriott in Seoul, South Korea. Julie's family emigrated from Korea to open a food store in Atlanta, Georgia, when she was a young girl. Her family instilled in her the key to success: to genuinely care for the customer as a person. At Marriott, the philosophy "take good care of the associate and they'll take good care of the customer" is paramount for her. Each day, Julie takes time to chat with associates in each department and send personal notes to any needing encouragement. Julie is a single mother with three young boys, but says, "Time spent out of my office may require me to work late or work at home to make up the time, but I think it's important."[1]

A few comments from other associates reinforce the value of her efforts:

> *"Julie really puts people first, always."* . . . *Su Jeong Choi, HR supervisor*
> *"She embraces everybody with love. Everyone feels that they can talk to her."* . . . *Hee Hwa Jung, café worker*
> *"She makes us feel comfortable, like we're coming home."* . . . *Tae Hwa Shin, pastry chef*[2]

As I've expressed an official eleventy-six times now, if the organization's collective efforts to engage employees and to care for them is solely measured by the tangible benefits (T1), then it is incumbent upon individual people—beginning with the *people* people (HR)—to create a real culture of care (T2) for those same employees.

Mentors, Role Models, Exemplars

Becoming a real People Person may require you to undergo a significant personal remodeling. The change might represent a complete night-to-day difference in your current attitude toward others. If so, it will demand constant attention and conscious, deliberate, daily choices that may seem insignificant on their own, but collectively comprise your progress in putting people first.

Saying a cheerful hello, asking if you can help, actually helping, boldly speaking up in a meeting, letting a simple offense roll off your back, using a little humor in an e-mail, sitting near strangers at lunch, being considerate to other drivers and many other day-to-day choices are examples of these little things.

It will be useful, if not absolutely necessary, to identify role models. As you've read this book, who has come to mind as an example of a People Person? At this point you may have thought of several coworkers, friends or family members that fit the bill. Observe their behaviors, how they communicate with others, the respect they show, the fun they have, how they stay genuine in any circumstance, and challenge yourself to start emulating those characteristics.

Don't worry that you'll lose yourself by copying someone else, particularly in cases where your personality requires major improvements anyway. The idea is not to entirely change who you are—that flies in the face of authenticity—it's to become the *best* you. More often than not, adopting a few qualities of others who have what you want or who are what you hope to become is the wisest approach to improving yourself without losing the essence of your identity. You are merely building on and bettering, not razing and reconstructing.

I have several peers that influence me in this way. One is able to speak frankly and openly with others about his opinion, positive or negative, in a way that hurts no feelings nor creates enmity. I am forever working on being more like him.

Another friend manages to be positive and nonjudgmental with literally everyone with whom he comes in contact, anytime, night or day. That level of consistency with other people is a quality I aspire to have.

My wife is constantly thinking of ways to help others in need and acting on them. This is a lifelong goal of mine—to be that outwardly focused—and she is my role model.

It helps me to have identified these people, to keep my eye on them, see what they do and try to do the same. It not only helps define the path I'm trying to take but shows me that it's humanly possible to take it.

But I also look to another source as an example to emulate. Earlier I mentioned that for this transformation to happen it need not be considered a quest for perfection or a form of worship by sacrifice and sanctification. But I would be remiss if I didn't acknowledge that this is, in fact, the case for me. My own personal desire to progress and develop as a People Person is both because of and dependent upon my own belief in deity. There is simply no way I could ever hope to become a truly decent human being without a lot of divine help. I'm that lame.

But I'm not alone. Most major personal conversions are the product of some kind of divine intervention or assistance. Do you know anyone who's been rehabilitated from deviant or antisocial behaviors? Someone who's determined to correct major flaws or radically improve personality faults, or who has broken free from harmful addictions? How many true stories have you read or seen depicted in movies in which hardened prisoners "find God" and radically change their very natures? I know a few people that fit that description.

Most of us probably aren't in need of a complete about-face inspired by a miraculous intervention from the man upstairs. But there's no question that when it comes to improving ourselves from the inside out, if we believe in a higher power, he'll definitely take an interest in helping us out.

The Holistic Approach—Take It Home

For many Aspirants, becoming a Type III People Person is a long-term commitment that requires persistent and consistent effort. Some may not be compelled enough to even care. For those who read this book and choose to live a people-first philosophy, it will require a holistic approach.

If you can make the effort to be gracious, charming and collaborative at work . . . take it home.

If you're able to speak honestly but with tact, share a laugh or create one, or take the time to appreciate someone's hard work . . . take it home.

If you are capable of cleaning up your break room mess or refilling the coffee pot at work . . . take it home.

If you're willing to forgive and forget inconsequential mistakes by others at work . . . take it home.

If you can manage to make it through an entire day without blowing your top and use only positive, appropriate language . . . take it home.

A People Person can be counted on for consistent character no matter where he or she may be. They listen. They laugh. They're sincere. They're not mean. They're nice.

Notes

Chapter Two

1. Marc Sessler, "Carlos Rogers: Jim Harbaugh 'a little crazy' with 49ers," NFL.com, June 27, 2012, www. nfl.com/news/story/09000d5d82a2a4df/article/carlos-rogers-jim-harbaugh-a-little-crazy-with-49ers.
2. Ibid.
3. Charlie L. Hardy and Mark Van Vugt, "Nice Guys Finish First: The Competitive Altruism Hypothesis," *Personality and Social Psychology Bulletin* 32 (2006): 1402.

Chapter Three

1. "Breaking Rules Makes You Seem Powerful," ScienceDaily, www.sciencedaily.com/releases/2011/05/110520092735.htm.
2. Gerben A. Van Kleef, Astrid C. Homan, Catrin Finkenauer, Seval Gündemir, and Eftychia Stamkou, "Breaking the Rules to Rise to Power: How Norm Violators Gain Power in the Eyes of Others," *Social Psychological and Personality Science,* January 26, 2011, DOI: 10.1177/1948550611398416.
3. "'Personality Genes' May Help Account for Longevity," Albert Einstein College of Medicine of Yeshiva University, May 24, 2012, www.einstein.yu.edu/news/releases/798/personality-genes-may-help-account-for-longevity.
4. Jenna Goudreau, "The 20 Best-Paying Jobs for People Persons," Forbes.com, February 28, 2012, www.forbes.com/sites/jennagoudreau/2012/02/28/the-20-best-paying-jobs-for-people-persons.
5. Ibid.
6. Ibid.

Chapter Four

1. "What Is a Great Workplace?," Great Place to Work Institute, www.greatplacetowork.com/our-approach/what-is-a-great-workplace.
2. Adam Bryant, "Google's Quest to Build a Better Boss," *New York Times,* March 12, 2011, www.nytimes.com/2011/03/13/business/13hire.html?pagewanted=1&_r+1&nl=todaysheadlines&emc=tha25.
3. Ultimate Software: Company Culture, www.ultimatesoftware.com/Ultimate_Company_Culture.
4. Brian Callahan, interview with the author, 2012.

Chapter Five

1. Danny Sullivan, "Microsoft Slams Google Privacy Changes with 'Putting People First' Ad Campaign," Marketing Land, February 1, 2012, http://marketingland.com/microsoft-slams-google-privacy-search-changes-with-putting-people-first-ad-campaign-4887.
2. Marriott: Core Values & Heritage, www.marriott.com/culture-and-values/core-values.mi (italics added).
3. Marriott: Stories of Excellence: Rick Collins, www.marriott.com/culture-and-values/RickCollins.mi.

Chapter Six

1. Auto Editors of Consumer Guide, "How Saturn Cars Work: Saturn Rethinks Car Manufacturing," HowStuffWorks, http://auto.howstuffworks.com/saturn-cars1.htm.
2. Auto Editors of Consumer Guide, "How Saturn Cars Work: Saturn Car Company: Buyer Satisfaction," HowStuffWorks,

http://auto.howstuffworks.com/saturn-cars4.htm.

3. Ibid.

4. Eknath Easwaran, *Gandhi the Man: The Story of His Transformation*, 3rd ed. (Tomales, CA: Nilgiri Press, 1997), 169.

Chapter Seven

1. Marcie Pitt-Catsouphes, Christina Matz-Costa, and Elyssa Besen, "Workplace Flexibility: Findings from the Age & Generations Study," The Sloan Center on Aging & Work at Boston College, Issue Brief 19 (January 2009), www.bc.edu/content/dam/files/research_sites/agingandwork/pdf/publications/IB19_WorkFlex.pdf.

2. Results-Only Work Environment (ROWE), www.gorowe.com.

3. "Road Rage Statistics," Stop Road Rage, June 2, 2012, www.stoproadrage.us/road-rage-statistics.

4. Philip Caulfield, "Car dealer retires, gives employees $1,000 for every year of service," *New York Daily News,* September 11, 2012, http://articles.nydailynews.com/2012-09-11/news/33768850_1_car-dealer-new-employees-dealership.

Chapter Eight

1. "In the News: Could I just finish, please?," *Education for Health* 16(1): 114–15, www.tandf.co.uk/journals, 2003, DOI: 10.1080/1357628031000066732.

2. Barbara Jones, "Burbank educator Rebecca Mieliwocki named National Teacher of the Year," *Daily Breeze,* April 23, 2012, www.dailybreeze.com/news/ci_20458633/burbank-educator-named-national-teacher-year.

3. Mark Memmott, "Teacher of the Year 'Known for Unconventional Techniques,'" NPR: The Two-Way, April 24, 2012, www.npr.org/blogs/the two-way/2012/04/24/151275785/teacher-of-the-year-known-for-unconventional-techniques.

4. Karen E. James, Lisa A. Burke, and Holly M. Hutchins, "Powerful or Pointless? Faculty Versus Student Perceptions of PowerPoint Use in Business Education," *Business Communication Quarterly* 69, no. 4 (December 2006): 374–96.

5. Jeffrey Kluger, "How America's Children Packed on the Pounds," *Time,* June 12, 2008, www.time.com/time/magazine/article/0,9171,1813985,00.html.

6. Mark Twain Quotations: Telephone, www.twainquotes.com/Telephone.html.

7. Zoe Fox, "31% of U.S. Adults Prefer to Be Reached by Text Message," Mashable Tech, September 19, 2011, http://mashable.com/2011/09/19/31-of-u-s-adults-prefer-to-be-reached-by-text-message-study.

8. Charlie White, "Texting Teens: Typing Replaces Talking," Mashable, July 2, 2011, http://mashable.com/2011/07/02/texting-teens-infographic.

9. Martha Irvine, "Text Messaging: Is Texting Ruining the Art of Conversation?," The Huffington Post, June 3, 2012, www.huffingtonpost.com/2012/06/03/text-messaging-texting-conversation_n_1566408.html.

10. Ibid.

11. Tom Espiner, "Survey: People skills valued over those for IT," CNET, December 14, 2007, http://news.cnet.com/Survey-People-skills-valued-over-those-for-IT/2100-1022_3-6222828.html.

12. Ibid.

13. Ibid.

Chapter Nine

1. Maria Marquart, "Study Finds Germans Incapable of Enjoying Life," Spiegel Online International, May 24, 2012, www.spiegel.de/international/zeitgeist/study-finds-germans-incapable-of-enjoying-life-a-834973.html.
2. Kurt Vonnegut, *A Man Without a Country* (New York: Seven Stories Press, 2005).
3. Martin Luther King Jr., *Strength to Love,* new ed. (Minneapolis, MN: Fortress Press, 1981), 35.
4. Steve Denning, "The Ten Happiest Jobs," Forbes, September 12, 2011, www.forbes.com/sites/stevedenning/2011/09/12/the-ten-happiest-jobs.
5. Annie Murphy Paul, "Your Brain on Fiction," *New York Times,* March 17, 2012, www.nytimes.com/2012/03/18/opinion/sunday/the-neuroscience-of-your-brain-on-fiction.html?pagewanted=all.
6. John P. Robinson and Steven Martin, "What Do Happy People Do?," *Social Indicators Research* 89.3 (December 2008): 565–71.
7. This research was done by Ipsos, a global market research company, and the results were presented in my previous book. See Adrian Gostick and Scott Christopher, *The Levity Effect: Why It Pays to Lighten Up* (Hoboken, NJ: John Wiley & Sons, 2008), 21.
8. Gostick and Christopher, *The Levity Effect,* 177.
9. Ibid., 14.
10. Melinda Smith, Gina Kemp, and Jeanne Segal, "Laughter Is the Best Medicine: The Health Benefits of Humor and Laughter," Helpguide.org, last updated September 2012, www.helpguide.org/life/humor_laughter_health.htm.

Chapter Ten

1. Marriott: Stories of Excellence: Julie Dongju Lee, www.marriott.com/culture-and-values/JulieDongjuLee.mi.
2. Ibid. These quotes are from the embedded video on this Web page titled "Julie Dongju Lee - 2012 J. Willard Marriott Award of Excellence Honoree."